The
FEMININE QUEST
FOR SUCCESS

The FEMININE QUEST FOR SUCCESS

HOW TO PROSPER IN BUSINESS AND BE TRUE TO YOURSELF

NANCY H. BANCROFT

Berrett-Koehler Publishers
San Francisco

Berrett-Koehler Publishers, Inc.
155 Montgomery Street
San Francisco, CA 94104-4109
Tel: (415) 288-0260   Fax: (415) 362-2512

ORDERING INFORMATION

Individual sales. Berrett-Koehler publications are available through most bookstores. They can also be ordered direct from Berrett-Koehler at the address above.

Quantity sales. Special discounts are available on quantity purchases by corporations, associations, and others. For details, contact the "Special Sales Department" at the Berrett-Koehler address above.

Orders for college textbook/course adoption use. Please contact Berrett-Koehler Publishers at the address above.

Orders by U.S. trade bookstores and wholesalers. Please contact Publishers Group West, 4065 Hollis Street, Box 8843, Emeryville, CA 94662. Tel: (510) 658-3453; 1-800-788-3123. Fax: (510) 658-1834

Printed in the United States of America

 Printed on acid-free and recycled paper that is composed of 50% recovered fiber, including 10% post consumer waste.

Library of Congress Cataloging-in-Publication Data

Bancroft, Nancy H., 1940–
        The feminine quest for success / by Nancy H. Bancroft.
             p.   cm.
        Includes bibliographical references and index.
        ISBN 1-881052-62-1 (alk. paper)
           1. Vocational guidance for women.   2. Success in business.
        3. Women in business.   4. Women—Communication.   5. Career
        development.   I. Title.
        HF5382.6.B36   1995
        650.14'082—dc20   95-34422
                                                                                          CIP

First Edition

99 98 97 96 95   10 9 8 7 6 5 4 3 2 1

Dedication

This book is dedicated to the forty-five women who openly shared their experiences with me. Their stories provided the inspiration for this book. I admire them all and cannot thank them enough for their generous help with this effort.

They are: Sharon Brownfield, Linda Burgess, Linda Cadigan, Nancy Cain, Tavia Campbell, Amy Connell, Susan Cornwall, Mary Davidson, Sarah Down, Susan Dryovage, Jerrie Fuller, Sue Gault, Graelin Geerkin, Jill Gribb, Helen Rolfe Ham, Nettie Ham, Shirley Harris, Maureen Hayes, Catherine Hillard, Sharon Hindus, Catherine Howells, Kate Johnson, Christie Jones, Leesa LeClair, Margaret Ledger, Linda Lerner, Rianna Merrill-Stone, Rox Neustadt, Jan Nickerson, Margie Pannell, Teresa Pappas, Kristin Paulson-Snyder, Marcia Polese, Dr. Lynne Reid, Paula Rhodes, Ann Marie Rosa, Ardis Smith, Linda Smith, Stephanie Speer, Stephanie Spong, Cheryl Suchors, Nancy Weeks, Saundra Wells-Davis, Jean Wentzell, and Roberta White-Smith.

Contents

Part Three: How to Increase Self-Alignment

Part Four: Changing the Business Environment

    Organizational Challenge   177
    • Fighting the Status Quo • A Systemic View • Feminine Pride

    Bibliography   191

    Index   195

    The Author   201

Preface

I grew up in the nineteen fifties, an era when women were inclined to accept well-defined nurturing roles in the world; for a working woman that meant nurse, secretary, or teacher. As a young girl I was trained by my mother to be helpful, pleasant, and accommodating. From those lessons I deduced that the way to survive and succeed was to pay close attention to everyone around me so that I could be aware of what they wanted or needed from me. By doing what was required, I could earn praise and be recognized as a good girl. Though I often rebelled and insisted on doing things my way, "proper" female behavior was more often rewarded.

In conjunction with my learned accommodating behavior, I also became afraid of those with control over me. I recall feeling helpless, fearful, and very angry. I learned two techniques that plague me today. I learned to be physically present yet emotionally absent. As a result I often felt I was not real, but that I was a figure in some video game yet to be invented.

In addition, I absorbed the skill of lashing out at people in ways that were, on the surface, amusing or completely rationalized. I might say in my early work years to a colleague, "I'm sorry you didn't realize I had already researched that topic and presented the conclusions to the boss." I would not have stinted at using a condescending tone to imply that the other was lazy and somewhat inept. I have struggled for years to conquer these tendencies. They have caused me a great deal of pain. I would disappear emotionally or strike out at someone. Then, I would spend hours deriding myself or, worse, not even notice I had hurt someone's feelings.

While there were obvious drawbacks to my childhood, it was not a bad one. I was given a great deal of freedom. I can remember my mother exclaiming with wonder, fear, and pride, "What are you doing at the top of that enormous tree?" As a young girl I knew intimately everyone's backyard—where the best blackberries were, where the frogs liked to rest in the afternoon, where the skunkweed grew, and how strong the current was at different spots in the river.

My younger years offered the advantage of helping me to develop exceptionally good intuitional skills—the ability to read the external environment—which have been very useful to me as a management consultant, manager, trainer, and writer.

The result of being encouraged to experiment led to my ability to take on many different projects and several career shifts. I had not, however, developed the ability to know what was true for me, let alone to act on that truth. I was reacting to my life as I perceived it rather than creating it.

The Working World

When I entered the workforce, I went about trying to understand the rules—how to act, what to say, how to succeed—in the same way I had approached the grownup world as a child. I thought, "I'm smart. I can learn this and then I'll be OK." I wanted to do it right, I wanted to be successful, and I needed the money. And I was successful. I earned a number of management positions that gave me considerable responsibility and influence. I enjoyed the challenge and the opportunity to bring about change. However, my experience was also confusing and frustrating.

By studying the work environment, I taught myself how to act and what to say. But the more I learned, the more I realized that I did not understand the success track. It seemed as though there was a secret code that I could not crack. My bosses were pleasant and always gave great reasons for my relatively low pay; they even tried to explain what I needed to do to earn the next promotion. But when I did those things, it still wasn't enough. I earned my promotions at a far slower pace than many of my male companions.

I was aware of the obvious sexist discrimination and the sexual harassment in the workplace, but I concentrated on being asexual, so the harassment was hardly ever aimed at me. It seemed to me that there was more to women being held back than just discrimination. Then I began to notice that my ways of approaching problems and interacting with co-workers were different from the ways men did these things. My male peers tended to think in terms of bulleted lists of essential points and they focused on achieving goals. I approached the same issues in terms of the interrelationships of the various factors and people involved, and I cared as much about how a problem was solved as whether it was solved.

After years of trying to "cover up" my own approach to business, I realized I was acting a role in order to fit in. I was bumping into the downside of my upbringing, which left my "inner world" out of synch with my "outer world." Having played a role for so long, I had little concept of who I was.

Self-Discovery

My growing awareness that I had lost myself led me to embark on a journey of self-discovery that spanned many years. I attended a number of personal growth workshops, read a great deal, and began to learn more and more about myself. Some of the insights were difficult to accept.

The first lesson was that I was not entirely the person I had believed myself to be. While I had thought of myself as a "good guy," I discovered that I could be sarcastic and demeaning. Learning about the dark side of my nature was painful, but also useful. Applying my insights to my career, I became aware that I was more competitive than I had realized.

I found I had to be careful about the way I spoke to my peers and subordinates; I was always careful with authority figures.

After years of searching and growing, I discovered that my inner feeling of satisfaction was dependent on following my own truth as a guideline for my actions. Being true to my feminine self led to far more business success than playing a role had. Amazing! And it also turned out to be the path to material success as well.

When I operate from my own truth, events seem to fall into place.

Early in my career, I was a project leader in an information systems development team. I became aware that an effort led by a colleague was in trouble and I volunteered to take it over, telling my boss some of the ideas I had for a different approach. I was surprised when he turned the project over to me and reassigned my peer—to his relief and the better use of his skills. I suggested to the customer that we put together a steering committee made up of people who would manage and use the new system. The purpose of this committee was to agree on its specifications and to oversee its development and implementation. At that time, this was a novel approach. I have since written a book about this method of systems development, and the process I described is widely followed.

Several aspects of my actions derived from following my own truth and bringing feminine qualities to work. I overcame my learned reluctance to imply that my colleague could not solve his own problems and followed my natural inclination to offer my help. The solution I proposed was a collaborative one that placed the direction of the project in the hands of the people who had the greatest interest in how the system would work. While I was available as the technical expert, I saw that role as only one of several of equal importance. Instead of taking control, responsibility, and credit, I shared these aspects of the project.

The project was very successful and led to my next promotion. Even more importantly, I was able to see the value of bringing my whole self to work and finding the courage to suggest my own novel ideas about caring for people and involving them in changes that affect them. When I stray from this sense of inner truth, I am less successful.

Some time ago, I was consulting with an organization in Atlanta. The president asked me to develop and run a team-building session for him and his staff. He wanted to address the issues that were keeping people from being truthful with each other. He and his staff agreed that they were ready for this level of individual disclosure. I interviewed each member of the staff, asking them what was working well in this executive group. While they were excited about the opportunities their business presented, there were, as there are in most groups, some difficulties. Staff members wanted more autonomy and felt that the president "lectured" them, not allowing them to speak their minds. One member in particular was pointed out as being a difficult person to work with.

I prepared an approach and discussed it with the president. He was hopeful that we would be able to help the "difficult" person see a better way to deliver critical information. The team was interested and challenged by the material presented and began to open up and voice some of the concerns troubling them. They were impressed by the openness of the president to hear them out.

At the end of the first day, I called the group's attention to some behaviors that were not helpful to them. I mentioned the behavior of the "difficult" person along with that of some others. Almost immediately I could feel in the pit of my stomach that I had made a mistake. I began to explain my rationale, but I could see from the faces in the room that I had not convinced them.

My motivation, and *I even knew it at the time*, was more to show how clever and observant I was than to serve their best interests. I had shifted from a deep desire to help my clients to a personal, superficial desire to move the group more quickly toward honesty than they could handle, even though that is what they had all asked for. Several people, including the president, began defending the one individual, although I had given a number of different examples. As a group, they colluded to protect the thorn in their sides.

Of course, my comments were disregarded and I had to work extra hard to regain their trust. Although I was right in what I had said, the portion of the truth that I ignored was the lack of readiness of the group to hear that information.

The Research Project

In recent years, I began considering why it was so difficult for me to hear my own truth and to act on it, and I started wondering if other working women had the same problem. At the same time, I became intrigued by the amount of money businesses invest to teach their employees "new" skills, such as collaboration, networking, teamwork, ability to deal with chaos, and caring for product, service, and customer. Most women have these skills, and yet businesses, operating in masculine terms, ignore them. (In using the term *business*, I include for-profit and nonprofit organizations as well as academia and government.)

This system is in place for historical reasons and not because of ill-intentioned people. The system came into being based on the vast predominance of men in the workforce and has continued because it worked. To consider the possibility that there are alternatives is to question the entire system—something that is frightening and difficult for any established structure to do.

One might argue that the increase of women, especially in the middle-management ranks, shows that businesses are doing their darndest to equalize opportunities for women. But this is *not the same* as making good use of the natural skills and attributes of women. What company after company has done is to hire and promote those women who are best able to emulate the men, thus keeping intact the essential masculine model of how business is carried out.

It seemed odd that this paradox could have escaped the notice of business leaders, and I wondered why they were not doing everything possible to change their corporate cultures to make better use of the skills their female employees already had. I wondered why the business culture has so little regard for wholeness in all employees.

To find the answers to my questions, I initiated a national research project that consisted of interviewing forty-five professional women with varied business experiences. I made sure there was a good demographic mix of women, which took into account factors such as their age, ethnicity, geographic location, level in their organization, and stage in their career. Their ages ranged from twenty-three to seventy-one, they had positions in a wide variety of business segments, many were very successful in traditional terms, and several had left the corporate structure to "do their own thing."

Included in the project were CEOs; founding members of firms; an associate engineer; a number of managers, including a first-level manager, marketing managers, general managers, and several program/project managers; some management consultants; a number of company vice presidents and presidents; a law professor; a hotel manager; two hospital administrators; several women in career transition; and the chair emeritus of the pathology department of a major hospital.

I designed the research to answer the following questions:

- What differences do women perceive between themselves and their male colleagues at work?
- What feminine characteristics can be applied to business?
- Which feminine characteristics do women suppress and why?
- What strategies do women use to be successful?
- How successful do women feel?
- How have some women been able to integrate their uniquely feminine characteristics into their jobs?

I did not predefine *feminine* (or *masculine*) for the respondents; I allowed them to define the terms themselves. Women generally agreed the feminine approach tends to emphasize the skills and attributes companies are so determined to train: collaboration, teamwork, shared power, seeing the whole picture, personal concern for the customer and the product, and other attributes.

In addition to the women, I interviewed five men in order to gain a male perspective on the same questions. I selected three who were familiar with my research and two who were not. The men included a principal in a consulting firm, the director of the organization development practice in another firm, a senior manager in the health care industry, the director of systems development and support in a major bank, and an observer/writer who works in the rapidly changing information systems technology field. I chose these men for their extensive experience in major corporations. The information from the men cannot be termed comprehensive, but it does add some breadth.

The stories I tell to illustrate each of the five success strategies are composites of actual situations related to me in my interviews. I have used fictitious names in all the examples in this book to provide anonymity. All of the quotes, however, are taken directly from my interviews and reflect women's true feelings and experiences.

From the research I learned a great deal about the courage of women who venture into corporate America. For many, the business environment is a hostile and often strange place. But women are learning to thrive there.

The Purpose of This Book

I borrowed the term *alignment* from the course "Leadership and Mastery," a product of Innovation Associates, located in Framingham, Massachusetts. The course describes what happens when the subgroups of an organization are moving in the same direction—aligned to the same master vision. The result of such alignment is a tremendous increase in effectiveness and vitality, since the parts are no longer fighting against each other to decide where they are going.

The same is true of an individual. When all parts of ourselves are aligned—all in communication and moving in the same direction—we have increased individual effectiveness, which leads to success in whatever endeavor we choose. In addition, we have an expanded sense of satisfaction with ourselves and our lives.

The main purpose of this book is to augment women's abilities to achieve these objectives for themselves and to provide challenge, support, and guidance in accomplishing that task. This book is also addressed to every man with a wife, daughter, or female colleague in the working world. It is my hope that men who read this book will reap the same benefits as women who read it and find support for their personal journeys toward self-alignment. But my primary focus is on the unique challenges women face. I hope that *The Feminine Quest for Success* will be useful reading for all women who work, whether in "big business," small business, the home, or as volunteers in community activities.

Acknowledgments

I wish to thank many people who were involved in the preparation of this book. I have dedicated the book to the forty-five women whom I interviewed; they were instrumental in forming my ideas for the model of the five success strategies. I also interviewed five men: Hanley Brite, Bobby Cameron, Bill Keena, Skip Paterson, and Joel Yanowitz. The discussions I had with each of them were enormously useful in balancing my viewpoint.

Several people were kind enough to read early drafts and provide useful comments. Thanks to Karen Oglivie, Carol Remz, and Stefania Calabi.

I also wish to thank several others for particular help. Joel Yanowitz, your help, ideas, and thoughtful discussion on the whole topic, and particularly on Systems Thinking, were invaluable. The deviations from this formal discipline are entirely my own decision. Steve Piersanti, thanks for pushing me to take my thinking to a deeper level. Judy Durzo, your ideas on the overall theme, gender differences, and the five strategies were well taken. Lin Barry, you provided enormously useful comments and edits, as did Sue Cornwall. Sue, thank you also for providing constant advice and support.

Finally, as always, I am touched by the tremendous encouragement and support given me by my husband, Hanley Brite.

NANCY H. BANCROFT

Evergreen, Colorado
January 1995

You need not apologize for being brilliant, talented, gorgeous, rich, or smart. Your success doesn't take away from anyone else's. It actually increases the possibility that others can have it too. Your money increases your capacity to give money to others, your joy increases your capacity to give joy to others, and your love increases your capacity to give love to others. Your playing small serves no one. It is a sick game. It is old thinking, and it is dire for the planet. Stop it immediately.

—Marianne Williamson
  A Woman's Worth

Introduction: Taking Courage
in Our Wholeness

It is time for women to take courage in their wholeness as females and to bring their femininity to light. It has never before been more critical that we find a better balance of feminine and masculine approaches in our society and thus our businesses.

Self-alignment—being true to yourself—is the key to finding that balance for both women and men. It also is a critical factor in determining both success in business and a sense of fulfillment in life. I use the term *self-alignment* to indicate increasing ability to discover and use all parts of ourselves to enhance our lives and the lives of others.

There are two aspects involved in an increase of self-alignment. One is discovery; the other is service. Some people are more introspective and prefer to invest in self-understanding. This knowledge invariably shifts their actions to augment their ability to be true to themselves. Others prefer to simply live the best life they can, judging their actions by the highest moral code they know. From their actions, they come to know themselves as people of integrity. Over time, the two aspects merge in a congruent person.

We may have to move patiently to effect a true measure of wholeness. Rapid change can frighten and threaten anyone, including ourselves. And we will not find it possible to eliminate the self- and system-imposed restrictions on feminine behavior overnight.

There is also another danger. To leap into expressing all the aspects of our personalities simply because we have given ourselves permission can result in our playing yet another role. To maintain integrity, we need to allow the buried aspects of ourselves to emerge gently, so that we continue to feel safe. We may find it necessary to re-experience in a safe environment the hidden reservoir of feelings that keep us stuck in old ways of thinking and acting.

With those caveats in mind, we need to remember that women bring a special set of qualities to business simply because of who they are. While women's training and natural tendencies toward caring, nurturing, relationships, and sharing of both success and failure have sometimes been characterized as weak or inconsequential, more and more frequently they are being revealed in a different light.

Here are some statements from women who have acquired a measure of self-alignment. The first is a woman who is a skilled consultant in organization development.

> The workplace was my salvation. I came from a quietly crazy family and grew up feeling unsafe. I invested much energy to overcome my circumstances. I'm a little sad about my need to do this.
>
> Only recently have I come to know myself and started to reclaim my feminine side. I depend on my intuition, but I keep it primarily to myself. Then I use my intellect to explain what I know. I find ways to join—to connect. I start my work with my clients by acknowledging exactly where they are. I have a special ability to do this. It is based on my ability to relate to others.

The next woman runs her own successful training business now after spending years working in large organizations. She is able to pick and choose projects because she has such a reputation for excellence.

I enjoyed the novelty of being a woman at the top of my class in college. This allowed me to think, be, express myself as a woman. I could be more colorful, for example. But I also had to learn to speak the business language. I tend to have multiple things going on in my head. Once people knew I knew what I was doing, they would accept that I would talk about five things at once. If they didn't know me, I tended to hold back on four of the things.

I didn't adapt very well. I got along in spite of being myself. This didn't help me. I would have gotten more promotions, but I generally don't constrain myself much. Well, maybe some in order to fit in. First I build a relationship with a boss or a colleague. Then I can be myself. I had one boss who ignored me. I told him I didn't like the way he treated me and that he was lumping me in with some other women he had hired who were not competent in their jobs. He improved but said I was "impossible" because I told him the truth. He did agree that my performance was excellent.

The next statement is from a young woman who moved to another country, spent six months learning the language, then applied for a high-level job. All the interviews for the position were conducted in her newly learned language, and she won the job—a job where she is in control of a new department.

I'm starting to be who I am now. I'm finding this is more important than anything. I lived behind a mask for the past seven to eight years. Now I don't care what I give up to be myself.

I like helping people to be really happy and I like creating effective places for people to work.

Most problems are in our own heads. I can't stand it when I see bright, competent women looking for authority figures to tell them what to do. I can't stand bosses. My happiest period was when my boss was seven thousand miles away. I had to figure my job out alone and I loved the independence and control. I turned around a whole women's organization. It was great!

Feminine Success Strategies

Over the years, success-minded women have devised various behavior strategies in order to succeed in the business world. Out of the interviews I conducted for this book five distinct Success Strategies emerged that women use to adapt to and succeed in the workplace. I have named each of these strategies according to the predominant behavior exhibited by the women who use it: Emulator, Trooper, Balancer, Seeker, and Integrator. A woman can be successful in traditional business terms using any of these strategies.

It is important to note that the business environment usually guides or forces women into the Emulator role because it is the most masculine of the strategies and has the most familiar feel for men. If you look like all the other red cells, the white cells will not attack you.

Following are brief descriptions of the five Success Strategies. Later in this book, each one will be explored in depth.

Emulators are competitive and driven to succeed, and they define success in traditional business terms. They choose the most aggressive men as role models, copy their behavior as closely as possible, and then focus on setting and reaching business goals that will place them in line for greater responsibilities and promotions. Of the forty-five women I interviewed, four were Emulators. In addition, five others said they had previously used this strategy.

Troopers are those who choose working hard as the main thrust of their strategy. Their motivation is to please others and to always have the right information. They are the ones often seen lugging around enormous piles of folders containing the research on whatever their current project might be. Ten of the forty-five women I interviewed were Troopers.

Balancers want it all. They want business success and a fully developed life with their families and friends. They may feel torn by their attempts to resolve what some see as a conflict between work and family life. At work, they offset their natural abilities with acquired skills so that they are able to be both collaborative and confrontational. A Balancer, for example, might courageously refuse a sought-after promotion if it required a move because she wants to keep her children in a school system they like. Of the forty-five interviewees, ten were Balancers.

Seekers are looking for self-alignment. While they are interested in a successful career, they define true success as the ability to know better who they are and to be able to express their full natures in the business world. Seekers explore a variety of different forms of learning to achieve their goals. There were eight Seekers in my group.

Integrators expect traditional success and generally find it. They have, or have developed, a strong sense of self-respect that results in excellent performance both at work and in the other facets of their lives. Beyond having acquired a balance of skills, they know and express themselves fully. They are, at once, assertive, powerful, competent, and feminine. Some women come to Integration very early in their lives; others take years to do so. I found seven I termed Early Integrators and six Late Integrators.

Relationships Among the Strategies

I have ordered the five success strategies based on the extent of self-alignment possessed by a woman. An Emulator is the least self-aligned and has developed only a portion of who she is in her quest for success, while an Integrator has developed more of her whole person and is able to call on more of her resources at will.

There is a difference between the first three—Emulator, Trooper, and Balancer—and the other two—Seeker and Integrator. They are all strategies to be sure, but the first three are adaptations women make to accommodate themselves to the business world. Each of these three attracts different types of personalities at first, although women find they may switch strategies if they are uncomfortable with one.

The last two are more akin to steps in personal or spiritual develop-ment. I believe that a valid tactic for approaching success at work, as in life, is to develop as solid a sense of ourselves as we can and to express that in visible ways. I have found self-alignment both a powerful process and a visible result of living a congruent life.

One may cycle through many strategies several times. One woman may go from Trooper to Seeker in order to move to Balancer. Another woman just starting to use the Integrator strategy may use the Emulator strategy to get through a meeting or a week. A Seeker may move to Integrator and in the process discover she still uses more of the Emulator or Trooper than she thought.

This model lends itself to contemplation of the nature of individu-als. I have been personally drawn to integration; thus employing that strategy is a desirable goal for me. My experience shows me that others who journey in that direction are authentic, satisfied, and generally effective in their lives. Thus, increasing integration is the bias of this book. But this approach is not for everyone. Other strategies may serve different individuals who at various times are pursuing different goals in their lives.

Using the Strategies as a Planning Tool

We can use a pie graph and an ellipse to represent how much of any of the strategies we use or have used at any point in our past and present (see Figure 1.1). We can also use these tools to image the way we want to use the five strategies in the future. With such a picture clearly in mind, we can focus our energies on changes we wish to make.

Women have responded to this model by saying they often find themselves using more than one strategy at any one time. One woman wrote the following to me.

> I think I have placed myself firmly in the middle of only three of the styles now. I've narrowed it down from all five. I now know that I have heavy Seeker going on. Some of that has to do with

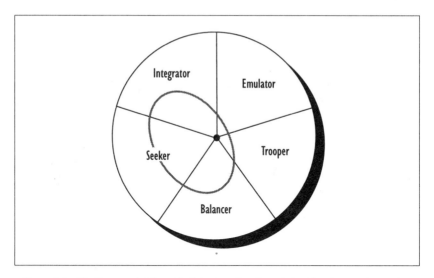

Figure I.1. Pie-Chart-and-Ellipse Tool for Imaging Use of the Five Success Strategies.

wanting to make some changes in my life now. The Integrator is where I want to be—my vision! And the Balancer makes up the difference.

The pie-chart-and-ellipse tool lets us glimpse our wholeness and view the process as well as the goal, our inclusiveness and collaborativeness, even our emotionalism and self-doubting. When the full range of options and abilities can be seen, hope and courage become available as well. Women who need to cast aside "helplessness" and stop playing the role of victim find they are able to do so. When we see how we have each participated in creating our current situation, we can each participate in changing it.

Increasing self-alignment will improve our effectiveness in meeting this challenge. It will allow us to feel confident about our feminine approaches, integrating them with the more masculine skills we have.

PART ONE

The Role of Self-Alignment at Work

1

The Double-Edged Sword:
Trade-offs and Contradictions at Work

F rederica, a district marketing manager in a large food distribution
company, is responsible for setting and achieving aggressive sales
goals in her district. She is a strong and capable woman who exudes confidence. One immediately believes she would be able to resolve any issue
or solve any problem.

At forty-one, despite her success, she felt dissatisfied with her position and wondered whether she should change jobs. She was unable to
say exactly what made her feel unfulfilled. Her work life just seemed to
be stale and boring. She felt conflicted because her job paid well and she
was good at it. Two years earlier she had experienced similar feelings of
discontent and had changed jobs. One problem was that most jobs in
her field tended to be about the same. Frederica considered a change in
careers instead, but could not think of any other type of work she really
wanted to do. In fact, she really did not want to start the learning curve
(or the salary range) over again. Feeling stuck and unfulfilled, she turned
to a friend for advice.

Her friend unwittingly launched Frederica into a self-discovery
process instead of a career change when he suggested she attend a year-
long series of management training seminars. Frederica agreed to attend

the seminars because she thought they would provide useful training regardless of what changes she eventually made. While she did learn many useful business skills, her real shift came as a result of her study group meetings. These evening meetings were intended to reinforce the seminar teachings and to provide interpersonal support and insight.

Over several months, the group interaction helped Frederica become aware of a previously unacknowledged layer of herself. She started listening to herself at a much deeper level. She found herself considering her role as a woman in business. She was horrified to realize she had eliminated some important parts of her personality in order to fit in with the working world's definition of how to act.

For example, she discovered she seldom took the time to listen to others with the intention of truly understanding their feelings and point of view. She habitually cut off people after a few words, since she believed she knew the gist of their communication. The group had given her some direct feedback whenever she used this tactic. She discovered that while it satisfied her need to get to the point, at the same time it left her feeling disconnected and out of place. She remembered the times in high school when she and her girlfriends used to spend hours talking. Those conversations, she recalled, had given her a feeling of connectedness, belonging, and wholeness. In adapting to the business world, she had eliminated opportunities to reexperience those feelings.

In addition, she realized that in moving so quickly to understand the point of any comment, she was not giving others the chance to express their feelings about the subject. She had little opportunity to know if they were excited, worried, frustrated, joyful, or challenged. As she reflected on this she realized with a jolt that of course the same was true of her communications to others. She spoke in brief sentences that comprised only the essential data and were flat in tone. Suddenly she realized why her small group seemed lost when she expressed her opinion about something they had all read. To her confusion, they often asked her why she felt a certain way or what the reading meant to her personally when she thought she had already communicated adequately.

These realizations gave her a feeling of panic at first. She feared that she might never be able to express her whole essence as a woman in her job. She began to understand that what she thought was a need to change jobs was in reality a deeper voice calling her to express herself more fully in whatever work she did.

At first she resisted her inner voice because it seemed to conflict with her perceived need to change jobs. She reasoned that she could not indulge in long meaningful conversations with everyone—how would the work get done? She was also afraid that if she paid attention to the voice, it would mean going through some mysterious mystical search. Frederica was not the type to go sit on top of a mountain and meditate; she just wanted to feel more satisfied with her job. To a friend she said, "I am so afraid I'll always be playing a role, yet I don't understand exactly what is missing—so how can I add it if I don't know what it is?"

But she persisted in pondering these questions, and as the year of meetings progressed, Frederica started noticing that her conversations with the local salespeople and their customers had begun to change in tone. More of her own excitement about her field was pushing through. Colleagues began to seek her out to request her opinions. She was told she seemed softer and more approachable. Frederica was delighted and surprised with these changes, since she felt she had done nothing more than consider her group's feedback and spend a little time attending to her own thoughts. These seemingly minor changes (in actuality not minor at all) led to a major shift in her perception of her working life. By the end of the year, Frederica was more satisfied with her job and with her life in general than she had been in a long time. In contrast to the year before, when she had sought advice from her friend, she felt excited and challenged by her work; she found she woke up in the morning with a desire to "get on with it."

Like Frederica, many women struggle with their feminine nature in the business world. They are taught in childhood that they must be accommodating, attentive, and pleasing to others in order to survive. For women to see themselves as powerful human beings requires the courage to face the truth of their femininity in the light of a society that considers the feminine to be soft, weak, and silly.

Many women (and most men) believe they must conform to the traditional business style in order to be perceived as having any potential for promotion. They are called to suppress (extinguish, if possible) their feminine energy. That this is impossible only makes some women try harder to accomplish it. "To be deemed 'successful' in our society, a woman has to become more like a man," observed Marilyn Mason (1991, 19).

Adapting to a hierarchical, patriarchal, aggressive culture is an issue for women and men alike. Numerous men acknowledge their own balance of masculine and feminine qualities and prefer to use all their traits, not just their masculinity. There are also those who question whether the model that predominates in business comprises the complete range of masculine traits. Masculinity, for example, includes a care-taking aspect—stewardship—that is underutilized in business today. (Read *Stewardship* by Peter Block [1993] for some positive examples.)

There are many women who, in trying to adapt, stress a masculine approach and hide their feminine qualities. The prevailing masculine paradigm constricts all of us.

Frederica's story, and the many others like it that you will find in these pages (including my own), illustrates the value of acknowledging the truth of our feminine nature and of having the courage to bring our whole selves to work. This book is about how women have had to hide their femininity in order to adapt to the predominantly masculine business style; it is about the differences between the masculine and feminine approaches to business; and it is about the power of showing our whole selves in all aspects of our lives.

A Woman's Style Is Not a Man's

Even though the current business culture is not one that naturally suits the feminine style, women have tried to fit in. They have learned to be assertive, to summarize their viewpoints, to make bottom-line decisions, and to dress in an asexual manner. But they have not learned how to be seen as men or how to ignore their natural tendencies, for example, to develop peer-to-peer relationships instead of hierarchical ones.

To be successful in business their own way, women must find and express themselves as strong, competent and confident, yet feminine, women. To become more like a man is a sham and will ultimately be recognized as such. "Let us imagine ourselves as selves, as at once striving and female," said Carolyn Heilbrun back in 1979 (p. 34). The key here is finding the true essence of who we really are, and that requires a search. It is as if we have made a deal to take our place in society; part of the deal is that we suppress or forget our essential self—who we really are. Thus, it is the game of life to rediscover who we are at the deepest level. The challenge to women is especially demanding because our society lacks so much of the feminine.

Women's natural style differs from that of men. Women are generally more in touch with feminine qualities, as men are more in touch with the masculine. This seems so normal to most of us that we forget to wonder why wholeness is not taught and celebrated more.

The feminine approach tends to be democratic, holistic, and process-oriented in the pursuit of results, while the masculine tends to be more hierarchical, linear, and goal-focused in seeking the same results. For example, women form relationships easily with individuals at all levels of their organization. When introduced to a new person or group, it is the first thing they attend to. Men are less interested in relationships for their own sake and more driven to form relationships with those in power or those with special information. Deborah Tannen in her book *You Just Don't Understand* (1990) termed their conversations "report talk," while women, she says, tend to prefer "rapport talk."

I recently saw Katie Couric interview Kathleen Turner on the *Today Show*. The two women—both strong, capable, and feminine—demonstrated in only a few minutes the typical way women operate when they are in touch with who they are and when they are in a situation that supports, even celebrates, that essence. The two women laughed together and talked about men and children while pitching Turner's latest movie. The objective was achieved and a great deal more as well. In the process, a relationship was established that was based on equality, power, and humor. All this in a few minutes.

The Feminine Conflict

For women who are raised to value connection, being helpful, equality with others, and caring, it is often a shock to be faced with a business environment (and a society) that operates as though these feminine attributes are useless, even disruptive. Because working women want to contribute to the success of the venture, their response is some form of accommodation, accompanied by an underlying feeling of giving up something important. When women abandon their own perspective and judgment to take on that of another, the result inevitably is some form of damage to their self-esteem. Deborah Tannen (1990), John Gray (1992), and Nina Boyd Krebs (1993), for example, talk about the results of being a woman living in a masculine world. However they appear from the outside, many women find it difficult to reach a balance that feels right.

One executive whom I interviewed told me she has struggled for years with how to be strong and influential and be a woman at the same time.

> I have a soft voice. This means that I can't be as loud as men.
> I can't have immediate impact. If I raise my voice, it sounds shrill.
> One time I was working with a man who was yelling and dismiss-
> ing what I had to say. I finally yelled back, which was what he was
> asking for, apparently, because he seemed to trust me after that
> and never yelled at me again.

It was difficult for this woman to use a form of communication that did not feel right to her. Eventually she did, but she remained frustrated about the incident.

Strength that originates from inner authority can, of course, be both soft and influential at the same time; these are not necessarily opposites. However, the prevailing opinion in the business world equates soft with weak.

> Yvonne had been a vice president and director of a marketing consulting firm. Petite and blond, she used to dress exclusively in mannishly designed suits and draw her hair back in a tight bun. She had also constricted her emotions because she had learned that expressing herself as a woman would be held against her. Indeed, she had found that her androgynous qualities made her a good negotiator, helped her get accepted, and protected her from being approached sexually. But after focusing on her career for many years, she reluctantly decided that she would have to leave the business world she enjoyed so much. She had come to realize that in her process of adapting to this environment she had made herself almost completely expressionless. Ultimately, Yvonne began to realize that she had nearly eliminated her feminine side:
>
> > *I noticed a split between my true self and what was required. As I developed my feminine side I found I couldn't hold it down anymore—I couldn't control it in the workplace. I had learned that in order to be successful I had to be expressionless and use logic, not intuition, to support my arguments. I don't believe I can find a place in a company where I can be my balanced self anymore.*
>
> At the time I spoke to her, Yvonne was excited about her new possibilities, yet sad about leaving the corporate world, which had given her so much challenge.

It may sound far-fetched to some that women, confident and capable in so many ways, could wind up so far removed from their ability to express themselves authentically. Yet others, myself among them, have acted in similar ways.

> For many years, I felt as though I had sent out a clone of myself to accomplish the necessary tasks. I played my role in as asexual

and assertive a way as possible. That I was in fact hard, cold, and frantic escaped my notice for several years. The only approach I could imagine was to attempt to control as much as possible, and that most particularly meant controlling my emotions.

I did not at that time have much understanding of what I had done to myself. I only knew that it didn't feel right, but I did not have enough perspective to see any other ways of acting. I felt very much alone because the only problems other women reported were ones of harassment and discrimination. I honestly did not feel either was the problem for me. I only felt as though I was not in touch with a portion of myself and totally incapable of finding a remedy for the situation. Over time I realized how constricting and conflicting this situation was for me. Eventually I also realized that it pervaded my whole life, where before I had only seen it in my work life.

In the sixties and seventies, there was little appreciation for the value of the feminine in the workplace. We focused on similarity—being the same as the men—and the result for many of us was elimination of a critical portion of ourselves.

I realized the best thing I could do was to discover my inner strengths and improve my self-esteem. Accomplishing these two goals, I thought, would allow me to show what I could do and improve my morale.

I have discovered that my process for self-discovery is to remain in ignorance of the truth for some period of time. During that time I unconsciously set up a situation to learn what I need to do to change. Finally, when the pain is intense enough and when I have some skills and direction, I let myself know what is actually true for me, proclaim earnestly that I cannot possibly change, and immediately make the changes required to take my next step. On the whole this is useful because I spare myself a certain degree of agony while at the same time gaining the skills to make the change.

I am working on shortening my whole cycle of learning. I have succeeded in reducing it from ten years to two months. It took me approximately ten years to be prepared to divorce; recently, after my mother died, I fell into a deep depression. Two months passed before I actually realized I had been depressed. Even though I had barely had the energy to get out of bed, I had attended several appointments with my acupuncturist, got a massage, and joined a grief support group. By the time I realized I was depressed, I had nearly worked my way out of it.

There are many companies and organizations within larger corporations that are working diligently to operate in a new, more balanced way. A male friend of mine has characterized this as corporate civil war. It is his opinion that this battle is between the old paradigm, or way of thinking, which is a slash-and-burn policy, and a new one, which is more holistic, sympathetic to the larger environment, and concerned about the importance of service. He drew my attention to a newspaper article that described a major shift in business books beginning in 1991; earlier books celebrated the successes of individuals who made millions of dollars and more recent ones espoused a more spiritual approach.

WHAT IS YOUR PROCESS FOR SELF-DISCOVERY?

- Make a list of the major life changes you have been through.
- What did you learn from each about yourself?
- When did you realize what you had learned? (Days, months, years later?)
- How painful was the change and the learning?
- Could you have learned in an easier way?
- Did the learning need to be repeated before you integrated it? How often or how frequently?
- What patterns can you see in the ways you learn about yourself? Are you satisfied with them or do you wish to change?

While it is exciting to feel these winds of change, for most people it is "the same old same-old." Managers as well as employees read the right books and speak the right words about valuing diversity and operating in a humane way. Some organizations are changing the way they operate; many are not as yet. As a change consultant I am often faced with a situation in which all parties agree—that they want to empower people, for example—but when a difficult decision has to be made, they cannot imagine letting their new culture actually work. They revert to the old way and make the decision at the upper-management level.

In such a climate, women in the business world are likely to feel bound by largely unspoken organizational norms as powerful as the wraps that bound the feet of proper Chinese women not too many years ago. No wonder they find themselves unable to show, or even feel, who they really are.

The Double-Edged Sword

Women possess many of the qualities sought by today's business environment, with its need for greater flexibility and connection; but the same business community that needs those skills constricts and deters the women who possess them. Simply being female is a double-edged sword; each advantage has a significant disadvantage connected with it. On the one hand, businesswomen who attempt to act like men may find that they are able to achieve what they set out to do—obtain information or make a sale, for example. On the other hand, successfully emulating men can have negative consequences. There is a very thin line of female behavior that is acceptable in the business world (sometimes the line is nonexistent). In most organizations, a woman must be assertive but not *too* assertive; she must be feminine but not *too* feminine; she must be supportive but not *too* supportive.

Until now, there has been no single successful strategy women could use to reduce the disadvantages of being feminine in the workplace. Each woman has had to adapt in her own way. These adaptations have included acting like men, getting along, compromising, and react-

THE DOUBLE-EDGED SWORD 13

DO YOU FEEL WOUNDED BY THE DOUBLE-EDGED SWORD?

- Do you put on a false face at work?
- Are you one person at home and another at work?
- Are your ideas ignored?
- Are those same ideas accepted when proposed by a man?
- Do you worry about your wardrobe presenting the right image? (Men do too, but do you worry about appearing too sexual or not feminine enough?)
- Are you the emotional sounding board for others in the office?
- Are you treated like a little girl or a favored daughter at work?
- Are you inclined (or pressured) to just act like "one of the boys"?

---

ing from situation to situation. Women are expected to operate within a narrow band of behavior, while men have much greater latitude. The consequences of wandering out of that narrow arena may be as obvious as ridicule and as subtle as not being considered for the next new project or promotion. Everyone loses when women are compelled by business norms to act in ways not natural to them, but women are especially constrained in the areas of influence, power, attention, and equality.

Influence

Influence is essential to success in an organization. To have one's plans and policies accepted means that one is valued. It also implies potential for advancement. The inability to influence others plagues women in their quest for success. Among the forces that keep women from being influential players are their tendency to placate and avoid conflict, being perceived as harmless, asking numerous questions, and being cast—and kept—in a support role. When a woman is seen as harmless or inoffensive, her attempts to influence others may be overlooked or rejected. The information and opinions she offers are discounted.

Women are often seen as having the right skills for filling support roles, especially positions in human resource management, in finance, and in information systems. Though women have some influence in these staff positions, it is very difficult for them to move from there to a line position, with responsibility for revenue-producing units. For women, managing support functions generally does not translate into line experience, which is essential for a move to executive leadership.

> Sally left a position as a midlevel manager for a Fortune 500 company because she knew she was far more capable than she was perceived to be by her management. Her contributions were often ignored and she had been passed over for promotions several times. She was told that she was a valuable employee because she could keep her subordinates happy and productive. Sally was astute enough to realize that she was seen as a pushover.
>
> Sally was offered a job in a small software company and shot to the top there. She had accepted the job because she discovered in the interview cycle that the company valued an open style, sharing of credit and responsibility, and intuitive decision making. She became an extremely effective project manager and member of the top management staff. Her peers attributed a large portion of the company's success to her ability to make the right deals. She found a situation in which her good ideas and ability to work with people were respected. Sally now has a great deal of influence.

Power

Real power, like influence, is essential to success in any organization. Real power is direct responsibility for managing others, and the more the better. Success in managing an organization with five thousand employees is considered better than managing one with fifty. Power is demonstrated by one's ability to direct, command, and control—but women are not perceived as being able to use power directly. Most women treat power differently than men do. Women are more likely than men to share their power and collaborate.

Women who share power for the purpose of building trust and teamwork are often perceived as weak by both subordinates and managers. Women usually direct others as peers rather than in a one-up/one-down hierarchy. They prefer to direct large companies on the basis of merit rather than position, relating to individuals on the basis of the importance of their ideas. This is amply illustrated by Sally Helgesen in her in-depth studies of four women CEOs described in *The Female Advantage* (1990).

In organizations in which women are in middle management positions, this tendency is often mistaken for a lack of ability to handle real power. Men, and some women, perceive this style as too soft. They fear it will lead to allowing someone inexperienced to take on a critical assignment, or taking too long to make a decision because of having to hear from everyone, or that the hard decisions may not be made at all in order to save someone's feelings.

> Sharon, manager of Advertising Operations, realigned her entire organization into teams and in so doing was able to provide better and more cost-effective service. The other managers, and her boss, were dubious about the change while it was in progress and dismissed her accomplishment afterwards despite the fact that the company was, at the time, seeking a consultant to teach collaboration techniques. Sharon was convinced that her approach was an excellent example of the desired direction for the company. She attempted to convince those around her of the long-term value of what she had accomplished, but was greatly frustrated that most preferred to keep to the old way. She was told that her organization was different than all the others in the company. This was offered both as implicit permission for her to continue as she had organized and as rationale for why no one else would try it.

Attention

Women do get attention, but it is more often due to their gender than to their accomplishments. Attractive women particularly are noticed. Anyone who wants to get ahead has to be visible, but visible women still may become corporate "decorations" or targets of outright harassment. It is important for an ambitious woman to distinguish herself from the competition for projects and promotions. Letting people know who she is—achieving visibility—is critical to moving up in an organization. For women, the attention is both necessary and problematic.

Marissa is a tall attractive redhead with intense blue eyes, now in her late thirties. Reflecting on her earlier experience as a young salesperson, she commented,

> It is easier for a woman to get in the door because men like a pretty face. You are pampered and nurtured more—picked up at the airport, wined and dined—but then, when the real business is done, you are discounted. You have to be twice as good to get the sale.

Equality

Many women feel they have to work harder and be better than men to get an equal chance at projects, promotions, rewards, and learning experiences—an equal chance at success. That they have to prove themselves more than men do is partially a result of generalized and unfocused feedback and the lack of effective mentoring from those with power.

Many women feel that good hard work will be seen and rewarded and like to do a job as completely as possible. Hard work is expected from both women and men, yet women are often exploited because they do work hard. An astute manager, it is said, looks to bolster the organization with a handful of hard-working women because the manager knows that they will complete the detail work that needs to be taken care of. While it is true that many men are also exploited, the numbers of women in such a position are far greater.

The Paradox: The Need for and Denial of
Feminine Business Acumen

To be successful, an employee must prove to others that she (or he) has "the right stuff"—a term borrowed from the early astronauts, who used it to indicate the ability to deal courageously and skillfully with the demons of outer space and speed. Up to now the right stuff has been almost exclusively in the province of masculine behaviors. This is not true anymore.

Joline Godfrey, in *Our Wildest Dreams* (1992, 4–5)—a wonderful book about women entrepreneurs—describes the new right stuff as "a set of values and qualities that actually bring the clichéd definition [of the right stuff] into question." The new qualities include, "ease in relationships and a drive for connection, a head, heart, and hands policy, appreciation of complexity and process and a desire for balance and self-awareness. For women, these qualities are, in part, the legacy of learning to survive in a frequently 'woman unfriendly' world."

I would add that they are also qualities that come naturally to women. In fact, these qualities reflect women's preferred way of operating.

When women limit themselves to the traditional criteria for success (position, power, aggressiveness, and the like) they limit their liveliness and wholeness. Women are deadening themselves by forcing themselves into the male-oriented business mold, and it is not necessary. Women can be forceful and confrontational but need to find a way to integrate feminine nature with the masculine skills required in business. Companies need feminine ingenuity and feminine success, whether or not they acknowledge it.

Most major corporations are involved in projects like Total Quality Management (TQM), reengineering, revitalizing, and so forth. These projects are geared to achieve increased teamwork, flatter and more flexible organizational structures, greater interpersonal skills, intraorganizational collaboration, and increased personal concern for both customer and product—all in an effort to improve business results.

The skills needed to achieve these objectives constitute the essence of the feminine style. That is, this is the way women tend to operate unless they have been sufficiently trained otherwise. It is also the way many men would prefer to operate if only their feminine side were not so actively discouraged.

And herein lies the paradox.

The business environment continues to disparage and even disown feminine qualities and, by implication, women. Felice Schwartz (1992, 217) states simply, "Despite the fact that they have the innate capabilities [needed to succeed], women are not being used as effectively as they might." She describes the business environment as "corrosive." It is costly not to provide an environment in which women can be themselves and be acknowledged for their contributions. By eliminating women from competition or by restricting women from expressing the full range of their skills and attributes, business has restricted its thinking to traditional solutions at a time when paradigm-breaking thinking is required. In clinging to these old strictures, businesses have limited their ability to choose the best of the best and allow them to succeed. That is exactly what most women at work want to do—be themselves and contribute. They are in a business environment that desperately needs their innate skills yet continues to rebuff them.

Why is it that while the skills and attitudes required in the new organization are feminine in nature, companies are not making their environments "woman friendly"? Corporations are spending vast sums of money to teach skills and instill values already held by many in the workforce while taking few strides to make the business environment more accepting of a balanced culture.

I set out to ask this question and cannot claim to have answered it. I have, however, discovered some interesting approaches that women (and, I imagine, men) have used to succeed and to make an impact on the workplace.

Women are not alone in their ability to make changes, but they are in the position of having more to gain and less to lose by changing the status quo. However, to think that women just need to be present in order for corporations to adopt an inclusive culture is a simplistic vision.

Women have found that they must work assiduously on two fronts. The first is to change the culture of business to a more balanced state. The second is to find and express themselves. This is the work that I term self-alignment: it is the process of discovering and using all our unique qualities. It requires us to establish a dialogue between our conscious mind, our subconscious, and our higher self. It is the way in which we can be ourselves and work most effectively in any organization. It is no coincidence that Gloria Steinem has come around to seeing the importance of this inner work, as shown in her book *Revolution from Within* (1992). I believe that working on the second will ultimately achieve the first. The data from the interviews I conducted support this conclusion.

Bringing About Change

Increasing self-alignment is work; it is a discipline—a discipline with enormous rewards for both the individual and society. Self-alignment—or, we might say, deep authenticity—increases a woman's ability to be successful in the world while increasing her own self-esteem. Women who are able to express themselves fully are powerful examples of the values inherent in the feminine style.

Expressing yourself is much more than expressing your emotions. It is finding a consistent, personal means of operating in the world that includes your feminine qualities. For men it is the process of finding a compassionate masculine way to operate. Finding that deeper self and expressing it is enormously powerful. The women who have tapped into even a portion of that power and have found the ability to make that self visible are outstanding leaders, mothers, and citizens. They are role models—women in a variety of roles who express the combination of feminine presence with a knowledge of how to get things done.

Once the search for expression is begun, the process will take on a life of its own, leading the seeker deeper and deeper into the mysteries of her own self. This is not a narcissistic process of self-absorption, however. Its purpose is to enable individuals to contribute their unique and special selves to the world—a world in extreme need of authenticity.

The strain of operating as a token woman, of fighting discrimination, and of wearing a persona that is not real has caused many women to reconsider the success strategies they have adopted. Women are ready to reclaim those aspects of feminine nature that they have had to set aside. In short, women have a unique set of skills and attributes desperately needed by the business world, and yet corporations remain corrosive places for women and ones that discourage women (and men) from using more than a narrow band of their complete selves.

2

A Model for Self-Alignment

Self-alignment is much discussed in spiritual, religious, and personal growth literature, but it is seldom mentioned as an aspect of the work life. Pursuing self-alignment as a personal goal while ignoring the full third of our lives spent at work, however, is meaningless. Our true nature is a whole and does not naturally segment into nice little boxes. Self-alignment must cross all aspects of our lives or it does not exist at all.

Self-alignment (other words would be *wholeness* or *authenticity*) is the increasing ability to discover and use all our qualities to enhance our lives and those of others. It is the ability to ensure that all aspects of ourselves are working together harmoniously. We find ourselves contributing, according to our abilities, in service to our environment as we understand it. In self-alignment we match doing with understanding. We are congruent with ourselves. This congruence reveals our ability to act in accordance with our deepest truth.

Communication within allows us to hear and act on the thoughts that emanate from our higher self. Others call this self-aspect "higher guidance," "inner teacher" or "the inner divinity." Martia Nelson in *Coming Home: The Return to True Self* (1993, 7) speaks of allowing higher guidance to be present in our lives. She says, "Its service is in assisting us in opening to our divine purpose and inner truth, then supporting us in integrating this alignment into the actions and experiences of our daily living. Our challenge throughout this process is to give up our tendency to deny our inner truth; only then are we really free to follow it."

When we are misaligned, we are in conflict with ourselves and with the world, and we may experience the conflict as unhappiness, anger, anxiety, friction, stress or as a variety of other negative feelings. It is as though the wheels on our car are out of alignment. We may not notice the difficulty at first, although the tires will. As time goes on the mis-alignment may worsen and surely we will notice a strange vibration, funny noises, or a decrease in miles per gallon.

When we take on a role that keeps us misaligned at work, such as a success strategy that is at odds with our true nature, we obviously cannot be fully effective. The negative emotions that derive from the conflict sap our energy, blur our focus, and overshadow our natural skills and talents. In the short run it may appear easier for women to dis-guise some aspects of our feminine nature in order to get along in busi-ness, but in the long run it is so self-destructive that it can curb sought-for success.

Benefits of Self-Alignment

Self-alignment, as illustrated by the story of this hospital administrator, is a key factor in achieving professional success.

> I was educated at a women's college. There I could grow without competition against males. I know who I am and what I'm about. I'm successful in being able to choose where I am willing to work. If your heart isn't in it, you can't succeed. I'm good enough to be able to be selective.
>
> I am highly intuitive. I understand that my boss needs facts and numbers. I give him those first, then he will tell me how he feels about something. He really loves the hospital. The feelings

really are there. Because I'm a female at the executive level, it makes it OK to talk about this stuff. This would not happen if I were at a lower level.

The self-assurance that evolves out of authenticity cannot be imitated. Confidence is compelling. It attracts others and inspires trust. The credibility that derives from that trust is perhaps the most important factor in a woman's business success. When a woman is trusted—is credible—colleagues are open to her ideas and more likely to respond with, for example, requested resources or ideas. Subordinates are more likely to expect success from a trusted and credible woman and will be drawn to help her achieve it. The positive attitude that derives from self-alignment becomes a self-fulfilling prophecy that makes even disappointments and downturns easier to overcome. Self-alignment does not guarantee success, it merely facilitates the process.

Unfortunately, personal integrity and learned business skills may still not be sufficient to invite business success for many women because in the business environment too few women are promoted to levels of significant responsibility. The playing field is still not level for women and minorities. To actually create a more open, collaborative business environment takes commitment and responsibility on all levels and in all employees.

It is my belief that women (and men) will both help themselves and improve the overall business climate when more of them choose to focus on their own self-alignment. However, maintaining self-alignment in a constricting business environment requires a balancing act. Women cannot afford to ignore external behavior that denies and denigrates them; they must be willing to speak out constructively when such behavior is overt and damaging.

External pressure, which can lead to feelings of frustration and anger, can upset the balance of self-alignment. It is important to keep anger in perspective and not be consumed by it. When employees are out of balance they may be tempted to select and lash out at one manager, treating him or her as the symbol of all discrimination and making that individual the recipient of all pent-up anger. Self-aligned employees are better able to respond appropriately to delays, disappointments, and disapproval. At times, it is appropriate to confront and, at other times, to be patient. Having greater congruence between our selves and our internal resources makes it easier to choose the suitable option.

> A midlevel manager who is quite self-aware told me a story of having to be out of work for a short time because her doctor had recommended a hysterectomy. She told her boss that she would be out and why. His embarrassed response was to assure her that in her case he would think no less of her. She laughed and told him that he showed real potential for joining the human race one day. This put him at ease, since banter was a part of their work relationship. She has found that humor is often a good way to treat such potentially difficult situations. She also has no difficulty with confrontation when it serves a purpose. In this case, she simply shook her head in bemused amazement at his stereotypical views of women.

The woman in this story was not afraid to show her confidence to her boss. But many women, regardless of their actual level of business skill or their belief in their own abilities, do not express confidence at work. Self-alignment increases any woman's self-perceived confidence and helps her find appropriate ways to express it. The greater a measure of self-alignment one has, the easier it is to remain confident of one's skills. I am speaking of true confidence, not the false image some women flaunt in order to fit in. This "female false bravado" is a common result of women trying too hard to play the role they assume is required and at the same time feeling a certain degree of insecurity. A truly confident and competent woman has access to an effectiveness that is honest and compelling. Her opinions will be sought, her style imitated, and she will be the most likely to be asked to take on greater levels of responsibility.

Daniela, a woman who works in the International Department of a major corporation, has acquired an easy confidence from her experiences in many different countries, although this quality was not easily achieved. Daniela is in great demand even in places not known to seek out women for their business advice. She is asked to attend high-level management meetings because she provides suggestions that are sound from a business perspective, yet show sensitivity to the local culture. She is able to defend business decisions, made with this balance in mind, to executives at corporate headquarters who are not as aware as she of the unique pressures managers in each country face.

From Daniela's own point of view, self-alignment brings with it an increased capacity to deal with and find vitality in all circumstances: "Early on I wondered what people saw in me that they asked me to do new things. I was driven by fear of failure rather than drawn by success. Something shifted to let me have an ego. I stopped being driven by fear and I allowed myself to use my creativity. Then, I finally experienced what people said about me. Today, I have developed more patience and acceptance of people just as they are. I have learned to be more tolerant without colluding with them. And I've learned that I don't have to change everybody."

Daniela is effective in her work largely because of her ability to be herself.

My Sources of Inspiration

I came to an understanding of self-alignment as the result of over twenty years of active searching for a way to be myself more completely. I was originally motivated by a sense of dis-ease and wanted to feel better about myself and my life. In the process of moving toward that goal, I discovered I wanted more than relief. I found I wanted to fulfill my mission in life and it was clear to me that doing that would require nothing less than complete knowledge of myself. I found I was willing to go anywhere, do anything, pay any price to find myself and to find the courage to express that essence freely in the world. I explored numerous sources that offered to teach me how to achieve this goal. You may find some or all of them to be useful.

The first major influence was the work of Robert Fritz, the founder of DMA, an organization that teaches individuals to use their higher self in creating the life they choose. I discovered Fritz in the late 1970s and attended several of his workshops, including formal DMA training. Fritz's approach is best stated in *The Path of Least Resistance* (1989, revised). Peter Senge freely credits Fritz for many of the elements in the discipline of Personal Mastery as set forth in *The Fifth Discipline* (1990). Fritz's ideas form the basis of a major module in much of the training delivered by Innovation Associates (IA), a forward-thinking consulting and training firm. Both Fritz and Senge were founding members of IA.

From the work of Fritz (1980, 1989), I learned that there is a way to create what I want. By holding steady my vision of, for example, the type of job I wanted, telling the truth about my "current reality" (that the job I had fell short of my preferred work), and being *willing to live with* the creative tension involved with the gap, I was able to generate the changes desired.

My search for my self-alignment was immensely aided by several sources that helped me to understand the notion of the higher self. Two that affected me deeply are quite dissimilar in approach. One is *Journey of Awakening* by Ram Dass (1978). I carried this book around for years, reading bits and pieces every day. It is a wonderful guide to meditation, quieting the mind, and coming into alignment with oneself. The work Ram Dass does continues to inspire me. His recent audiotape series *Spiritual Awakening* (1993) is excellent. Through his insights, I have come to know that I can access my deepest resources and that I am more than I (usually) think I am. Besides being a speaker, author, consultant, wife and mother, I am connected to others and to a higher source of wisdom. I am more than the roles I play.

I was also influenced profoundly by *Global Mind Change* by Willis

Harman (1988). Harman is president of the Institute of Noetic Sciences, a group dedicated to the "all-inclusive ways of knowing, which form the basis for how we see ourselves, each other, and the world." This book challenges the prevailing scientific paradigm at the heart of how we know anything to be true. I have felt supported personally and professionally by the realization that not everything that is true can be proven scientifically.

Most recently I have discovered several books that have been pivotal to increasing my understanding of what I term self-alignment. I have already quoted from *Coming Home: The Return to True Self*, by Martia Nelson. Nelson also offers workshops and individual sessions designed to help individuals increase access to their inner wisdom.

Three others I found inspiring are *Where Two Worlds Touch*, by Gloria Karpinski, and *You Can Have It All*, by Arnold M. Patent. Both speak of ways to discover and access universal wisdom. In addition, *Do What You Love, The Money Will Follow*, by Marsha Sinetar, provides practical advice to people interested in finding work that is truly their "right livelihood."

I have also attended numerous workshops and conferences, all of which added, in some measure, to my understanding and appreciation of self-alignment.

When I started to find my strengths and build my self-esteem, I had started to improve my level of self-alignment. As I continued this process, I found far more to know about myself than I had previously imagined. I found the search led me to that level in myself where there is no difference between people, where we are all souls with different lessons to learn. Increasing my self-alignment turned into a sometimes painful but always joyful process.

Self-Alignment Is a Process

From moment to moment, the ability to be in tune with oneself shifts, making self-alignment a dynamic and often elusive process. Self-alignment is a creative process—not an event. It is more an urge than a destination, since destination implies that once you have arrived, there is nothing more to do. Nor can it be considered a continuous state that, once achieved, exists without change from that time forward. In this process we find ourselves increasing our understanding and appreciation of the value of our selves. Achieving self-alignment consistently is a lifelong discipline; that is, it is a body of work that requires commitment to the development of its skills. Peter Senge (1990, 141) says of this discipline that it "goes beyond competence and skills, though it is grounded in competence and skills. It goes beyond spiritual unfolding or opening, although it requires spiritual growth. It means approaching one's life as a creative work."

Carl Rogers, the preeminent psychologist, explores this process in his classic work, *On Becoming a Person* (1961). He says of people who are successful in finding their potential for growth (self-alignment) that they "seem to move toward more openly being a process, a fluidity, a changing. They are not disturbed to find that they are not the same from day to day, that they do not always hold the same feelings toward a given experience or person, that they are not always consistent. They are in flux, and seem more content to continue in this flowing current" (p. 171).

For women, this growth process is analogous to the change from adolescence to womanhood. One day we are little girls and the next we feel all grown up, then back again. For several years, to our own dismay and that of our parents, we go back and forth. Later, we mostly feel adult except for occasional days when we feel little again. Eventually we realize that we have not even questioned being an adult for years, and we find that we can act like children occasionally without worrying about whether it is appropriate. Further, we continue to redefine for ourselves what "adult" means to us.

> I am a short woman. For years, even after I married, I had the feeling that the grownups let me stay up late to attend a party. I would look up at others and feel like a little girl. Over the years, as I gained professional success, it diminished but would still reappear from time to time. In the early 1980s, I conducted a consulting project in Puerto Rico and had to make a number of trips to

that country. There the people are shorter than the average U.S. citizen, and I found I liked the feeling of looking people straight in the eye. As I told my friends and colleagues about my experiences in Puerto Rico, I realized that I had forgotten about my earlier feeling of being a little girl and that it had been several years since I had felt so small.

So it is with self-alignment. We go back and forth—one day being in communication with our inner selves, the next feeling out of synch, and the next back together again. Eventually the times of inner harmony increase until we live major portions of our lives open to our shifting feelings and self-knowledge. And even on days when we are not in synch, we are able to smile at ourselves, knowing we will soon realign.

It is hard to retain a concrete sense of our self-alignment when disaster strikes. It is even difficult to keep it amidst the everyday stresses and demands on our time and attention. Being in self-alignment helps us maintain a feeling of well-being, regardless of circumstances. Several women in my study said they were surprised at how calmly they had accepted difficulty when they experienced a major catastrophe. They found self-alignment was particularly helpful in difficult times, especially those times when they were rejected by others for some business reason.

Women, being generally so attuned to others, easily accept the idea that a negative comment about our skills, or a rumor that distorts a remark we have made, or even someone's facial expression of distaste when we enter a room, means that we are headed for disaster. Self-alignment opens the doors to another way.

One self-aligned executive told me that she had found a way to turn the loss of a major client—what to her would have normally been a devastating event—into a way to strengthen her connections with other clients who were more in tune with what she had to offer. The original contract had been a good money maker, but had taken her away from the work that really excited her. Her inner wisdom reminded her that she was just fine without this source of income and that this event presented her with more of an opportunity than a crisis. Rather than become upset, she became excited about allowing herself to do more of the work she loved.

The Structure of Self-Alignment

Self-alignment can be seen as establishing a dialogue between three aspects or spheres of self-awareness: the conscious mind, the subconscious, and the higher self. The greater and more positive the communication between the three, the greater the self-alignment. In order to be true to ourselves, these three, not merely the conscious mind, are the ones to which we must listen.

Many writers and philosophers discuss these three elements. In *Higher Creativity: Liberating the Unconscious for Breakthrough Insights* Willis Harman and Howard Rheingold (1984, 153) state, "Integration of the personality implies alignment of conscious with supraconscious choice, so that the whole of one's being—subconscious, conscious, and supraconscious—is conflict free and all directed toward the same end." The book demystifies the creative process and focuses on the role of the subconscious in that effort.

Robert Fritz, in the *DMA Course Manual* (1980, 35), uses similar terms—"unconscious," "conscious," and "superconscious." He agrees that the key to creating the sort of life you want lies in the ability to use what he calls the unconscious. Further, he says that the superconscious is connected to universal mind/wisdom, or God. "Your own true nature and purpose are important influences in your life. . . . Frustration arises when the true nature of self is resisted. The superconscious contains the ideal and perfect prototype which is indeed your own true nature." In other words, you already exist in your perfect state. You just need to access what is already there.

In *Stepping Free of Limiting Patterns* (1992), Pat McCallum again uses essentially the same terminology and provides practical assistance for communicating clearly with the subconscious. The purpose of the steps she describes is to eliminate the feelings, thoughts, and behaviors that keep us from achieving the goals we set for ourselves.

The Conscious Mind

The conscious mind is the part of you that gets up in the morning, pulls on your panty hose, and goes to work. It is what we use to make decisions (although there is another way), do our taxes, prepare a presentation, and make dinner.

Joseph Luft defines the conscious mind as the combination of our behavior, feelings, and motivation, and in a classic work, *Of Human Interaction* (1969, 13), he describes a construct he developed with Harry Ingham called the Johari Window (see Figure 2.1). I've used this model numerous times over the years. In a personal conversation, Dr. Luft told me the model is enjoying a resurgence of interest. He also told me a most interesting story regarding the word "Johari." He invented the name as a combination of his and his colleague's first names; however, he has

Figure 2.1. The Johari Window.
Reprinted by permission, from Luft, *Of Human Interaction*, 13.

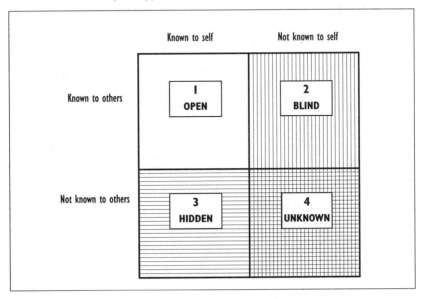

since learned that in Swahili the word means "the essence of things" and in Sanskrit, even more appropriately, it means "the God who sees within."

Figure 2.1 can help us think of our behavior, feelings, and motivation in terms of four quadrants. Quadrant 1 is the open area, the part of us that is apparent. It is useful, over time, to seek to expand this quadrant. This is what is commonly called pushing at the edges of your comfort zone. Quadrant 2 is the blind area, where we are known to others but not to ourselves. This may be illustrated by a person who discovers something about themselves—that they get angry or fearful, for example, when someone implies their work is not perfect. The individual may have thought she or he was good at taking this type of criticism when in fact the response was defensiveness. In such cases, nearly everyone except that person knows how he or she reacts to feedback, while the individual in question is in the dark.

Quadrant 3 is the hidden area, that collection of thoughts and feelings we keep, successfully, to ourselves. I know that my colleague is often rude and arrogant to others; however, she is not ready to hear this from me. Perhaps an appropriate time will occur when I can deliver this feedback. Perhaps not.

Finally, quadrant 4, the unknown area, is made up of those thoughts, feelings, and even behaviors that are unknown both to the self and to others.

It is useful to understand the nature of our conscious mind as we approach the next element, the subconscious. Not everything that is operative, even on the surface, is known to us or to others. Increasing self-knowledge will enlarge quadrant 1 and simultaneously shrink the other three areas.

The subconscious can assist us in opening ourselves to the inner knowledge that we have, for various reasons, barred from our conscious minds. We have constant and instant communication with the subconscious. Our inner dialogue, or self-talk, is the key to accessing the power of the subconscious to help us create our life circumstances the way we want them.

Barriers and Paths to the Subconscious

Confusingly enough, negative self-talk and the underlying beliefs that support it are both the barriers and the pathways to the subconscious. Understanding and defusing these two troublesome elements is critical to moving deeper into ourselves to find our hidden inner wisdom.

By "self-talk," I mean the little voice in our heads that constantly comments on everything we do, see, or experience. If, on reading this, you are asking yourself, "What little voice?" you have just become aware of it. With some of our messages we reward or inspire ourselves: *I really came out looking good in this meeting. I'll have to remember that closing; the style seems to work for me.* Sometimes we criticize ourselves with our messages: *That was dumb; I knew I shouldn't bring up that topic in this meeting.* And some of our messages just reinforce bad habits: *I was right all along and this proves it* (after repeating a situation that always turns out badly).

When the communication channel is not fully open, what we hear as self-talk is principally superficial messages like *I'm a good person, so why do people exclude me?* or *I'm really smart and skilled, so I know I can do this big job.* Just beneath these messages, however, there is also a somewhat quieter voice with which we often indict ourselves: *I'm afraid I'm not a very likable person* or *I wonder if I'm just fooling everyone about how well I can do this job.*

These indictments generally expose our underlying contradictory beliefs, which we must acknowledge and deal with as part of the current reality in any situation. Peter Senge (1990, 156) says, "Most of us hold one of two contradictory beliefs that limit our ability to create what we really want. The more common is belief in our powerlessness—our inability to bring into being all the things we really care about. The other belief centers on unworthiness—that we do not deserve to have what we truly desire." I have found it enormously comforting to realize I am not alone in harboring beliefs that have constrained my ability to improve my self-esteem.

These messages reflect the long-term beliefs we have about ourselves, which usually develop unconsciously during childhood. While we have both positive and negative beliefs, the negative ones will more often cause us difficulties: *I believe I'm really not a good person* or *I believe I'm not very smart or competent.* When we hold these underlying contradictory beliefs, regardless of our more positive feelings, we will eventually act in a way to prove the negative belief is true.

To begin to communicate with the subconscious, it is helpful to realize that these beliefs may be inaccurate or incomplete. Robert Fritz (1980) says it is not useful to examine whether a belief is true or not—you will create circumstances to prove your beliefs automatically. Instead, it is useful to identify them and consider them as opinions that may or may not be true. Until I recognized these beliefs as opinions of my conscious mind, I could not hear my higher self clearly. The static was so loud that I was incapable of hearing the softer deeper voice.

> Mary, an account executive for an ad agency, was dominated by a belief that she was not articulate. She felt as though her words ran over each other as she tried to convey the complexity of the ideas she intuitively understood. Because of this belief, she avoided making presentations about her work, which was creative and at times groundbreaking. A mentor pointed out to Mary that this was holding her back in her career. Mary joined Toastmasters for some support and there developed the confidence to present her ideas. Soon she was sought out by many organizations to deliver speeches and was even paid to be a "keynoter."
>
> When Mary realized her long-held belief did not reflect the truth about herself, she was released from an inner restriction. In truth, she was very articulate when she was talking about something that really excited her.

Beliefs like Mary's exist even for people who are closely aligned with themselves. Ram Dass (1993) talks about them as destructive parts of himself that turn up from time to time. They never completely disappear, but they do lose their power to affect our actions as we confront them. When we notice them, it is like greeting an old friend: "Oh, hello, self-doubt. Back again, I see!"

Confronting the myths that emanate from our self-talk and under-lying contradictory beliefs is a key step toward greater self-alignment. It is only when we can accept ourselves, warts and all, that we are able to change those things we wish to change. Dealing with the "dark side" will take the bogeyman out of the closet and into the well-lit room where we can assess his power. Generally he is smaller and less potent than we thought.

Our negative self-talk and contradictory beliefs constrict us; they are barriers to greater understanding. At the same time, they provide an excellent indication of areas for growth. Yet growth can be daunting and even painful, while fooling ourselves that we are always happy and good may actually make us feel quite comfortable for a while. These short-term good feelings, however, are mere shadows of the positive feelings we can have if we move beyond our conscious mind to hearing the sub-conscious speak the truth of the higher self.

The Subconscious

We can think of the subconscious as our servant: that is, it serves by cre-ating what we tell it to create. However, as I learned in the workshop "Leadership and Mastery," it is not all that easy, since we often send conflicting messages. We say, for example, "I really would like to get promoted into my old manager's job." And the subconscious says, "Yes, great idea!" All would be fine if we left it at that; however, the subcon-scious also pays equal attention to other messages related to the same subject. So when we also deliver messages from the conscious mind such as, "I am worried I don't have what it takes to operate at that orga-nizational level," and "I don't think my boss's boss likes me," and "Women don't seem to move up in this organization very quickly," the subconscious says "Yes" with equal earnestness. The subconscious then concludes you really *don't* want the promotion and does not work at achieving it.

The subconscious also communicates in the other direction, if we will listen. It can be heard as intuition or premonition. Many call it simply the inner voice. John Bradshaw, in *Healing the Shame That Binds You* (1988, 185), says, "In beginning this work of confronting and changing our inner voices, it's imperative that you realize how powerful these voices can be." We should not dismiss this powerful force, but work to make it an ally.

The subconscious often delivers messages to the conscious mind that are the instructions for achieving a goal previously chosen. It may, for example, say, "You should probably go and talk to your old boss about her boss and how to approach him" or "Boy, you sure are talking yourself down these days, it's time for a good dose of self-esteem."

When we come to the subconscious, we may experience it as words or a feeling; it may be kinesthetic, or we may simply recognize it intuitively as truth. An example on a more superficial level may prove useful. This journey toward greater authenticity is best taken in an easy frame of mind.

> Alice was jolted into hearing her subconscious by an outside event. She was given a promotion, but the new job was in Europe, so she had to decide whether she was willing to relocate. She really wanted the job and the experience it would give her and decided to take it. In doing this, she had to give up almost everything known and familiar.
>
> Alice placed her beloved car on the market and called a mover. But she soon realized something was troubling her. She reviewed the sequence of her decisions. Each felt right until she came to the car. Here, obviously, was the problem.
>
> Keeping the car was not a logical choice, but she realized that it represented a constant that she could not give up. She decided to keep the car and instantly felt a sense of happiness and relief. Furthermore, all the little details of making her life-changing move began to fall into place. The fact that she had decided to sell the car had been a barrier to the whole process, and now that it was removed, things flowed smoothly.

When we allow the subconscious to play its part in the dialogue, we sense that we are kind or lighthearted or competent, but how can we know when we hear the inner message "I am a good person" that it is the true message of the subconscious and not a superficial message of the conscious mind? The words are the same, but the feeling quality is not.

Superficial messages feel as though they are coming only from the intellect, while we sense, at a feeling and an emotional level, when our subconscious is delivering truth. The sense of relief and ease Alice experienced was her clue that she had accessed a fundamental truth for herself. When events flow smoothly and easily, it is often because we are in synch with ourselves. And this is as true for inconsequential decisions—such as whether to keep the car—as for major ones, such as whether to move to another country.

Our ability to hear our subconscious will be reflected in the outer circumstances of our lives. I told the story of Frederica at the beginning of Chapter One. She was the district marketing manager who attended a year-long management training program that helped her explore ways to be more her feminine self at work. As her self-talk changed, Frederica found that her relationships with her colleagues and clients also began to change in ways that were extremely satisfying to her. In other words, she was able to see the effects of greater congruence reflected in her outer life circumstances.

The expression of self-alignment is different for different people. The appearance of order may mean nothing in terms of a woman's state of self-alignment. Her relationships may be smooth and caring. Her children may be well dressed. Her house may be immaculate, and she may be trusted and respected in her job. For one woman, this will be evidence to her that her life is deeply satisfying. Another may wonder why, if she has done everything "right," she suffers from feelings of loss or a desire for something more. While we cannot make assumptions about the outer circumstances of another, we can look to our own lives for clues about our self-alignment. When the answers to the boxed questions in this section are truly satisfying, we can know we are moving in the right direction.

QUESTIONS TO ASK ABOUT YOUR SUBCONSCIOUS

- Do you feel supported by your messages to yourself?
- How often do you criticize yourself?
- What are the contradictory messages that get in your way?
- How often have you heard your subconscious?
- How do you experience your subconscious?
- Are those incoming messages the ones that guide your life?

Our social self is how we are known to others. While the subconscious and higher self are our being, the outer expression is our doing. What we do in life—that is, our actions—results from playing the several roles we each have; it may or may not reflect who we really are, our being, our inner selves. People who have opened this inner channel of communication report that their external lives accurately manifest who they are and therefore satisfy them. They are doing their being. Martia Nelson (1993, 58) says that your self-alignment leads to greater effectiveness in the world. "When you have a life that is based on who you truly are, no amount of change can shake you, no amount of uncertainty can bring instability."

Author Jan Nickerson (1993) provides a good example of someone who is inner-directed. Jan has extensive experience in business and has held several senior positions in finance. Her most recent job transition demonstrates the power of knowing oneself when looking for the perfect job.

Because of downsizing in her company, Jan was told that her job required only the "power of a popgun" and she was "a twelve-gauge." Jan saw this as an opportunity to find another and better job and to use the search for her own growth: "Now my voice came from deep within my body, not from my head. Now my voice could fully express the freedom that I felt to explore and create my future"(p. 140). Jan saw the search process as similar to planting a garden. "I watered and nurtured my garden, in the beginning with only the faith that something was growing. And then the garden started to blossom—one plant after another, and another" (p. 146). Finally Jan was offered a job that fit every one of her criteria.

Even before her dream job found her, Jan began to see the outward results of her commitment to her inner truth. She found job offers extended to her, each one closer and closer to her ideal until the final perfect one.

The Higher Self

The higher self is our life guide; we can best access it through the subconscious. We cannot rely on the conscious mind to make this connection for us—in fact, it is likely to get in the way of that process. The higher self will reveal to us our mission in life. It is also the channel to the Universal Wisdom, or God. Arnold M. Patent, in *You Can Have It All* (1991, 7), writes of this connection with the "Infinite Intelligence of the Universe." He says, "This Intelligence is available to each of us—in truth, It is a part of us. Accepting the fact that we have access to this Intelligence allows us to open ourselves to It. This Intelligence contacts us through our intuition. We feel It and hear It when our conscious minds are quiet and we are in a state of calmness and peacefulness."

Self-alignment, the ability to use all our resources, opens up a dialogue with aspects of ourselves that will help us to make the decisions that are truly best for us and that serve others. June Singer, in *Seeing Through the Visible World* (1990, xxii), notes, "there is another way of knowing: the way of the *soul*. This kind of knowing has been called *gnosis* since ancient times, to distinguish it from the kind of knowledge that comes from intellect and reason alone."

> MaryJo is a consultant and trainer in a large and still-growing health care company. She has a brilliant mind and is able to size up most situations in very short order. She is also extremely creative and comes up with ideas for her clients that amaze other consultants.

They wonder at her audacity to say and do some of the things that result in getting the clients to address the real underlying issues that divide and distress them.

In her earlier years, MaryJo was not particularly successful. She was hired because people sensed she had excellent insights; however, she often frightened and confused them. Because she could sense the reality of any situation so quickly, she would start telling people what was going on very early in the process. They would become defensive (partly because she had gone right to the sore spot) and assume that she could not be correct, since she had only been given a small amount of data. Her colleagues began to use her to assess the situation. She would tell them her insights and they would continue with the client without her.

Not very pleased about this, MaryJo came to realize that because she did not feel safe, she did not share enough of herself to make others feel safe. She started to delve deeper into herself. She began to access the wisdom she intuitively always knew she had. Soon she began to see that her clients avoided the difficult issues because they found them overwhelming. She found ways to lead them to see what she saw. Sometimes it was months before a client was prepared to see that an associate had to be fired or that key managers were losing trust in her or him, or that the client's own style was a major part of the company's difficulties.

MaryJo's life today is quite different. She is sought after and respected. She loves her business and feels as though she is making a contribution to the world through the help she gives others.

When MaryJo decided it was time to change, she started by working on her self-talk. She paid attention to what she said to herself. She discovered that she often called herself "idiot" and "dummy." On going deeper, she realized she carried with her a constant feeling of fear that someone would find out she was faking it. The combination of her fear and her insights kept her in a constant state of tension, which began to explain some physical difficulties—stiffness and headaches. MaryJo joined a stretching class at the local health club. As her body loosened up and became more flexible, so did her messages to herself. Soon she was saying "nice going" and "you can be afraid and still move on."

She learned to trust herself and began to feel comfortable with her intuition. Then she was able to relax and see that her clients needed support and a sense of safety, especially when dealing with extremely difficult issues. Her style became a reflection of her higher self. If she had focused only on her behavior, trying to learn new tricks to communicate her insights, she would not have been as successful.

Humans have asked the same questions for generations: "Who am I?" "What am I striving for?" "Why am I here?" We would all love to be given the answers, yet it seems that the process of life is to answer them for ourselves. None of us may ever learn the full nature of why we have been placed on the planet, but the benefits of searching are motivation enough to open up the communication between the conscious mind, the subconscious, and our higher self.

Establishing the dialogue between the three aspects of ourselves will change the nature of our self-talk and underlying contradictory belief structures, which are the signposts that show us the nature of the internal communication. When our self-communication becomes clearer, we find that the self-talk and belief structures become more positive and open. Simultaneously, we find that our outer circumstances begin to shift and our lives begin to reflect more closely who we are. Thus we are engaged in a positive reinforcing circle that constantly adds to our ability to effectively access and use all our resources.

To assess how open our channel is to the higher self, we can ask ourselves about what we want to get out of life, what calls to us, what ignites our passion. We also need to identify painful or frightening elements in our lives that we need to face and cope with.

When all aspects of ourselves are working together toward the same

---

QUESTIONS TO ASK ABOUT YOUR HIGHER SELF

- What do I truly want from life?
- What excites or challenges me?
- How often do I give myself time to be quiet and listen?
- What calls to me?
- What am I passionate about?
- What am I pushing away that I need to accept?

---

goal, we are self-aligned. That goal may be directed by our mission in life. At the most superficial level, life mission is expressed as wishes: "All I want is to win the lottery, sail around the world, and never work another day in my life." But there are deeper levels of mission, the deepest of which, like the subconscious, we do not typically hear in our head. We are more likely to feel or sense their presence, especially when we find ourselves making choices that we cannot explain.

Marcia's life mission emerged for her as a shift in perspective. She was working as a graphic designer, but the work was boring her. She decided that she had to make a change and thought that she had to find a new career. About that time a friend told her about a trip he was planning. He was going to spend a year bicycling around China and perhaps other countries as well. He invited her to join him. Something about the plan lit a fire in Marcia. Within three weeks she left her job, sublet her apartment, packed a few clothes, and got a passport. She had no bicycle, no experience in camping or dealing with foreign countries, and most especially, no money. She went anyway.

A year later when Marcia returned home, tanned, strong, and with outstanding negotiation skills that she had developed dealing with another culture, she realized that her mission had been to find a new way to live her life, not a new career. Her purpose, she realized, was to live her life in such a way that she was constantly in alignment with herself. What she did was not as important as how she did it. She went back to graphic design, but with an entirely new attitude and sense of her own worth and liveliness.

Most of us do not need to take a year off and bicycle around China in order to access our higher selves or our life mission. Marcia's insight took her a year, but the shift in perspective can begin in an instant, as it did for Ann, whose story you will find in greater detail in Chapters Seven and Eight.

Today Ann is a relaxed, warm, thoughtful woman who some years ago found that she had become cold and harsh in her dealings with others at work. In her attempt to fit into the business culture, she had developed a style that was abrupt. One day she gave some feedback to an employee, believing that she was being helpful, albeit critical. The employee looked at her sadly and asked her how she could be so unsupportive and distant in the way she offered feedback. In that moment, Ann realized she was not being true to herself when she was at work. She became aware of the difference between the abrupt manager she was at work and the kind woman she knew herself to be at heart. She embarked on a process of self-discovery and began to make the changes that eventually led to a greater ability to show her kinder side at work without subverting her business skills.

Most women have a desire to contribute to the world, each in our own way. By establishing a dialogue between our conscious minds, our subconscious, and our higher selves, we can find out what our way is. This activity verifies the process of expressing who we are as individuals and as women.

3

Different Genders: Different Styles

As each of us moves toward a deeper understanding and expression of our own self-alignment, we will find a greater expression of feminine qualities coming into focus. Currently, both men and women are badly out of balance. We are trapped by a prevailing cultural norm that reinforces a limited view of masculine attributes and devalues the feminine.

In the world of work, a greater emphasis on the feminine will provide greater collaboration, teamwork, holistic thinking, and personal concern for the customer and for the product. Feminine traits are needed to make businesses more flexible, adaptive, and organizationally flatter, allowing individuals to take responsibility for themselves and their work. Thus the behavioral attributes that women bring to business are valuable and useful. They increase collaboration, networking, and teamwork; they ease interpersonal relationships; they facilitate the organization's ability to deal with chaos; they bring greater emphasis to caring for the product or the customer.

Women and Men Are Different

The three most currently visible theorists on gender differences are Anne Wilson Schaef (1981), Carol Gilligan (1982), and Deborah

Tannen (1990). Each provides a powerful picture of the differences between the genders. John Gray's (1992) popular book *Men Are from Mars, Women Are from Venus* addresses the issues of intimate relationships from a psychologist's perspective. Other male authors address gender differences solely in the context of business.

Schaef describes our prevailing masculine system as characterized by rational thought, a dependence on empirical evidence, and a power hierarchy. In contrast, Schaef defines the feminine system as one in which people are peers unless proven otherwise, power is limitless, leadership is for the purpose of enabling others, rules are developed to increase individual freedom, and thought is multivariant and multidimensional.

Tannen focuses on communication. She claims that men communicate in order to convey status. The primary means of establishing one's position is by telling others what to do or by giving advice. Conflict is also used to establish status and as such it is sought and even enjoyed. Men prefer public speaking or "report talk," which is a way of sharing information on objective topics like politics and sports. Women prefer "rapport talk" that conveys connection, intimacy, and understanding. Women's talk focuses on maintaining a complex network of friendships, minimizing differences, reaching consensus, and avoiding the appearance of superiority. Women seek to minimize conflict through compromise and avoid it altogether when possible.

Gilligan bases her theory on the finding that girls have a different psychosocial experience than boys do because they are parented by a person of the same gender. For boys, growing up is defined as separation, while for girls, it is defined as attachment. This different route to maturity explains why males are threatened by intimacy, females by separation. As adults, women make moral judgments according to an "ethic of care," while men are guided by an "ethic of rights."

Despite the variations in focus, all three authors construe the differences between women and men to be developmental—the results of cultural immersion. Socialization predisposes each gender to act in specific ways, and each gender's different psychology has a significant impact on the work environment. Business is conducted in a masculine mode. It is assumed that women need to study books and attend workshops on the details of the masculine business behavior in order to better imitate it.

Researchers in the behavioral sciences have also jumped into the fray. In a work on brain studies, Anne Moir and David Jessel (1989) summarize growing evidence that the brains of women and men look and function differently:

> While the male brain gives men the edge in dealing with things and theorems, the female brain is organized to respond more sensitively to all sensory stimuli. Women do better than men on tests of verbal ability. Females are equipped to receive a wider range of sensory information, to connect and relate that information with greater facility, to place a primacy on personal relationships, and to communicate. Cultural influences may reinforce these strengths, but the advantages are innate. Scientific studies in various cultures indicate that women tend to be more peaceful, intuitive, sensitive to sensory stimuli, and relational than are men.

One of the most compelling studies of innate gender differences is one that compares same-age, same-sex pairs of infants, children, young adults, and older adults. This study, which has been widely cited, was a research project that Deborah Tannen participated in and to which she devotes an entire chapter of *You Just Don't Understand* (1990). In all cases, individuals have more similarity with others of their own gender—regardless of age—than they do with others of the same age but opposite gender. For example, little girls are more like adult women than they are like little boys of the same age.

Women and Men Are Also the Same

There are also many similarities between women and men. Testing and research demonstrate that the goals and many of the behaviors of professionals are the same, regardless of gender. One woman professional whom I interviewed claims that she sees no difference between women and men in the ways in which they perform their jobs. She found other indicators, such as psychological type, to provide more useful information than gender. Determining whether her employees process information internally or prefer to discuss the issue with others before coming to a decision is of more help to her in managing her subordinates than their gender.

Many studies of executive personality, intelligence, and problem-solving behavior reveal greater similarities than differences. *Breaking the Glass Ceiling* (Morrison et al., 1992) as well as Ann Morrison's later work support this viewpoint. These studies, however, are based on personality and behavior profiles, which examine a tendency toward a personality construct or a skill. These profiles are not designed to measure *how* one uses a given attribute or skill. Both women and men are competitive and wish to succeed. As managers, they plan, direct, monitor, and measure the performance of others. The crucial point is that how they carry out these tasks or express their tendencies may be very different.

For years, when looking for jobs, women have argued that there is no difference in ability between women and men, and women ought to be paid the same for the same work. This argument has contributed to women moving closer to equality. However, since women have not reached professional parity with men yet, many women still prefer to stress the similarities between the genders rather than the differences. Some of the similarities have occurred as women entering the workforce have been required to adopt the masculine way of operating and thinking. It is small wonder that women and men solve problems in a similar way, since the business culture adheres to the masculine system described by Schaef. While business problem-solving techniques come and go, they all share a consistent dependence on logic, concrete data, and linear process.

So Which Is It—Same or Different?

Ultimately, men and women are both similar and different. Certainly women are as motivated to succeed as men, and certainly women and men can have similar personalities. It has even been acknowledged (finally) that women are as intelligent as men. However, that there are similarities in behavior and performance does not negate the fact that there are essential differences between the genders. Regardless of cause, they exist.

Reading Schaef, Tannen, Gilligan, or other authors can help women articulate what they previously understood only intuitively about themselves. It is helpful to be able to say "Aha, now I know why I act or speak the way I do, I'm not crazy and there are plenty of others who face the same issues."

While the differences women bring to the workplace are valuable and useful in today's environment, we must be cautious about swinging the pendulum to the other end and assuming women will solve all the problems in business with their feminine leadership skills. This is a fallacy and a setup. To hire women and sit back waiting for them to change the culture is naive and damaging to both women and to the change effort.

One male manager told me that he and his management team would at times discuss how to achieve greater equality for women, particularly in the management ranks. The difficulty, he said, is that women are so visible, everything they do is under a microscope. "You can hide a man," he said, referring to the ability to cover up a man's mistakes, "but you can't hide a woman." Until you can also "hide a woman" it will remain difficult for women to be themselves, especially at the higher corporate levels.

And with regard to solving problems in the workplace, women do not have all the answers, any more than men do; a balance of skills and approaches by both women and men is necessary. The business world is neglecting a potential benefit as it continues to require women to behave like men when it could encourage them to be powerful, competent women. Companies that encourage their employees, women and men, to be themselves and that encourage managers to use the variety of attributes available in their staffs, will be more likely to survive in the current and future business environment. To hold to one way of operating, and thereby to eliminate from consideration those who operate differently, is to greatly diminish the ability to creatively solve complex business problems.

What Are the Differences?

I asked my forty-five female and five male interviewees to list attributes characteristic of themselves and of their colleagues. Almost all of the women had a great deal to say in response to the question; the men had very little to say. I suspect that either the men were trying to be careful and correct in their answers or they saw such vast differences they found it impossible to generalize. The sample size of men, however, is too small to draw any conclusions in this regard.

Some women were careful to say that not all of their co-workers fit the generalizations they were about to give. Some men, the women emphasized, are process-oriented, empathetic, and collaborative, while many women are aggressive, confident, and competitive. Overall, the picture I received is more reflective of the differences between masculine and feminine styles than between men and women.

The descriptions from the women were complete, complex, and rich in detail. This rich detail is important for two reasons: First, it shows that women have more innate talent to offer than is normally apparent in the business world. Second, this detailed picture validates the feminine qualities and their value to the business world. This validation should encourage women to find and express themselves more fully. Many women know themselves to be far more three-dimensional than they are allowed to appear in the business world.

The list of attributes that follows is a distillation of that research. It is supported in large measure by much that is written about the subject, including works by the authors mentioned earlier.

I list these contrasting qualities because many women have never seen the value of their innate attributes in a business setting. As you read through this list and the following discussion of each quality, you might find it useful to ask yourself to what extent you are capable of operating

---

CONTRASTING TRAITS DISTILLED FROM THE RESEARCH

Feminine	Masculine
Holistic	Linear
Process-oriented	Result-oriented
Inclusive	Hierarchical
Collaborative	Territorial
Emotional	Stoic
Self-doubting	Confident

---

in the feminine way and to what extent your culture encourages these qualities. (All quotations in the following sections are from female interviewees.)

Holistic

The feminine approach is to carefully consider, analyze, and make decisions on the basis of multiple factors. These factors include the feelings of the people involved, probable consequences, implications, interpersonal relationships, and the decision maker's intuitive "take" on the situation, along with surface data, such as who did what to whom, what the business results were, and whether the product was delivered on time. We can call this a holistic or systemic view of events, situations, and organizations. By *holistic*, I mean containing all the elements of the whole. A major part of this larger view is family life.

One executive noted, "I find I have to mentally 'go away' to get my ideas—to find them. Men think in boxes, highlights, and flowcharts. I don't think that way. It's more like clouds, feelings, and paragraphs—narrative rather than bullets."

A young research engineer reported, "Women are very thorough. If something is wrong they would see it and fix it. Women see the whole picture. I like to address a problem quickly."

A manufacturing line manager observed, "I notice that women

tend to look at the whole picture instead of one element. To be success-ful, I believe you have to look at the process. I am clear with my group as to where we need to go; we work together and then I have to lay out the whole plan. I have to be careful to break it down into small details, because most of them don't see the overall aspects the way I do."

Close to 50 percent of the women surveyed found it to be more characteristic for women than men to include this detailed data in their decision making.

Several women talked about how they wait and gather as much information as possible before making a decision. For some, this was a tactic to ensure the decision would not be criticized; for others, it was a need to include all the relevant data.

Seeing the whole picture is not the same thing as seeing the big picture. For many, thinking and planning strategically is a skill they need to learn. One executive noted, "I had to apply myself to develop the ability to think strategically; it did not come naturally to me. In my experience, women easily take in all the details about a situation, but the situations they analyze with detail tend to be of the day-to-day type. Using long-term strategic vision is something women have to learn."

The feminine approach is to hold in mind, and to balance, many details of the job, task, or goal, including the interrelationships, time sequence, and impact of each. Many of these details are qualitative. One woman, a managing director of a major furniture manufacturer, con-fessed that her boss, the CEO, often confers with her to see what he missed in a meeting. He relies on her to tell him what *really* happened. She picks up the small details he tends to miss.

Linear

My interviewees characterize the linear masculine approach as wanting hard data and preferring bullets, boxes, and concrete bottom-line information. Another aspect of this approach is to see things dual-istically: right or wrong, win or lose, in or out. Men tend to reduce problem situations to a few critical dimensions in order to more easily resolve them. They want to identify the two or three most important issues, deal with them, and move on. They are action-oriented, want to get on to the next issue or problem, and thus tend to make decisions faster than women do.

This approach is the counterpoint to the feminine holistic approach—the ability to see the whole picture. The information men typically leave out is the nonparticular. Much of what men see as the whole picture is the spoken, definite, concrete information. In the earlier example, the male CEO wanted his female managing director to collect the unspoken, felt information, which he knew generally escaped him. She said, "Men often miss what's really happening. I don't think that way. They miss what is *meant* even when they hear what was *said*."

Nina Boyd Krebs (1993, 282) speaks to the same point: "Women tend to see many sides to an issue and take them into consideration in making decisions. While men certainly have the capacity to do the same thing, the traditional masculine approach relies more on rules, the law, or agreed-upon steps to arrive at a solution."

> Recently I told my husband about a business situation and in an effort to understand and help he asked me for the five reasons the client was headed for trouble. I gave him two bullet points and then lapsed into a holistic description of the interrelationships of the issues. I had difficulty conceiving of the issue in terms of bullet points, and he got lost in the description.

This exchange reminded me of the descriptions Tannen (1990) and Gray (1992) give of the differences in women's and men's conversation. Men, they both report, will more often hear the problem and then offer suggestions for resolving it. Women, in their research, will more often listen intently and then offer consolation and similar examples.

Process-Oriented
The feminine approach is to give great care and attention to the process of doing a task, accomplishing a goal, or implementing a change.

Women tend to balance the process along with a concern for the content or result. The managing director who briefs her boss after meetings notes that the details she observes are often more related to the process of the event than to the content. She may inform him, for example, that his financial manager is unhappy with the long-range plan, not because he said anything, but because of his demeanor or because he raised objections about a related topic or because he suddenly left the room ostensibly to take a break.

> Women look at the process and ask how we can fix it rather than assume the people are the problem.

> I've observed that women executives are oriented to people and process. When they talk about subjects such as improving customer service, they put things like culture high on the list. By *culture* they mean how people really get things done and what gets in their way—the people/process stuff.

Seeing the whole picture and being respectful of the process required to accomplish a task lead women to generally let events unfold in their natural time, although this does not have to be an inordinate amount of time.

> I wait to see what will emerge in a situation; then I know how to get done what I have to do.

> Women are naturally good administrators. They are practical, keep several balls in the air, decide what needs to be done, and then get on with it.

Result-Oriented

The masculine approach is to go for the big win. Many men have the ability to focus intensely on a goal and do whatever it takes to reach it. They tend to see details as extraneous and to concentrate on results, with only moderate attention to process. Krebs (1993, 64) reports: "Masculine-style persistence paints with a broad brush; it tends to be aggressive and goal-oriented. It's designed to accomplish something that is clear and obtainable: to win a heart or a game, to solve an engineering problem, to make a point. When a man is persistent, you know it."

> Men are focused. They are action-oriented, jumping in to do something—anything. They generally have a solution at hand for any problem. They are looking to set up the "sure deal."

> Women consider how things will affect others' lives overall. If men think about that, they don't communicate it.

> Men have a singular determination; they focus on one goal. I admire men for that, but the process approach also has value.

Many women regard the masculine focus on results as missing the whole picture—acquiring only partial data and deciding without regard for the implications. Yet women agree that the result-oriented approach produces decisions more quickly. While taking immediate action may have limitations, certainly there are times when it is the preferable approach. Many women expressed an admiration for those who are able to focus intently, disregard extraneous details, and complete a task, solve a problem, or win in business consistently.

Inclusive

The inclusive feminine approach, as defined by my interviews, is to make personal connections with others in business, both for individual satisfaction and to smooth the process. When making decisions, those who use the inclusive approach tend to consider the feelings, needs, and desires of others.

Women, in general, relate easily to people at any level. They can develop trust, confidence, rapport, and respect when allowed in. They are generally supportive, empathetic, and good listeners. And they do not take these behaviors for granted. Women tend to place great value and emphasis on their relationships, yet my interviewees did not single out this trait as representing the most significant difference between men and women. My conclusion is that they perceive their ability to be inclusive as integrated with the other feminine traits. From the feminine perspective, then, the *whole* picture includes the feelings of others; the significant details include other people's needs; and the tasks that must be balanced include relational ones. Connection is central to the feminine approach.

Aburdene and Naisbitt (1992, 71) state that women will be successful in business because of their inclusive approach: "Women business owners are more likely to succeed, says Janet Harris-Lange, president of the National Association of Women Business Owners, because women admit they need help and surround themselves with good people."

Women are particularly good as members or leaders of teams because they provide a sort of relational glue that binds the members together.

Said one project manager, "Women work cooperatively. They check their egos at the door. They bring more personal concerns and interests to the job. Women include social talk in their meetings, particularly when the attendees are other women. Women relate to others—it's the first thing that happens in any situation."

A hospital administrator said, "What helps me to be successful is feeling things—using my empathy. I am dealing with a lot of staff people. You have to be willing to deal with all the emotions. I place value on the subtleties, like if there's an illness in the family. People appreciate my input and they trust me."

Some people perceive questions regarding personal issues as weak or irrelevant, but personal interest can help situations go more smoothly. One man confessed that he likes women who "do the female relationship thing," since it helps people work better together.

Women compete with one another over many things; however, in a working relationship, they may be reluctant to single themselves out as better than the other. This may explain why women often avoid opportunities to sell themselves, even when their accomplishments justify such action. "Women complete a task, but don't go after the recognition," observed one young manager. Many women agree with her, but some think of it as adhering to a moral imperative, while others blame themselves for not being more assertive. In either case, it is clear that women find it difficult to inform others of their successful achievements. Successful women learn to let others know of their accomplishments, but for most it does not come naturally.

Some women have a tendency to accept authority figures and experts at face value. One interviewee said, "Women can paint people into corners and jab at them," implying that women do not seem to understand how things are done (at least in the male system) and that consequently they may cause hard feelings unintentionally. This "jabbing" is one of the dark sides of the feminine approach. A colleague at an organization comprising primarily women reports that they all "made nice" when face to face, yet found numerous ways to cut one another down in other situations. Women may indeed resort to nastiness and undercutting more often than men do in a business conflict. This could result from a sense of insecurity or it could be another way to compete—but without drawing obvious attention to oneself. It contrasts vividly with the more masculine tactic of confidently presenting firm assertions (that may or may not be supportable).

Hierarchical

The masculine hierarchical approach includes one or another version of the "old boy" network—the system characterized by men's room and golf course politics. It involves "you take care of me and I'll take care of you" deals, and yielding to the position and opinion of people above you.

Most men know their place in the hierarchy and constantly strive to improve that position. They generally recognize who has power and who is weak. Men may be uncomfortable in teams where power and decisions are shared. Even those who would prefer not to operate according to this pattern find themselves drawn into it.

This hierarchical trait, above all, is the one that typifies the "old school" of business. Most business leaders today realize that a more egalitarian collaborative form of structure is needed, espousing political, financial, and social equality for all, but many who have already proven themselves by achieving some form of success in the old system would like to apply the change to others and not themselves.

Several years ago, I was brought in as a consultant for an automotive business. My client produced components for its parent company, a big automobile manufacturer. The president of the component company asked me to assess the success of their self-empowered work team efforts. Implementing self-empowered work teams is a popular approach used by organizational consultants today. It requires a change in organizational structure (into teams) and then training the individuals to work collaboratively to solve problems, make decisions, assign work, train newcomers, and the like. It means giving power to the individuals in the team to decide how to achieve team goals as well as goals they set for themselves. In practice it means each member of the team takes it upon herself or himself to do whatever is necessary to make the team successful.

The component company had been in the process of changing their operating structure and teaching team techniques for problem solving for three years but still had not seen the hoped-for results. There had been a slight improvement in quality but little improvement in volume. The time to manufacture each component was lower than expected and, significantly, managers at the level above the team leaders found themselves involved in such issues as discipline, when they had thought the teams would take care of those issues themselves. The overall measure of production was lower than it had been before they began the change.

I spoke to people at all levels in the organization and presented my findings. Self-empowered work teams began and ended on the shop floor. The management (exclusively male) was solidly hierar-chical and was adamant about remaining that way. As a result, the teams were not truly responsible for their actions; management was. Individually, team members (including a high percentage of women) tried to live up to the new norms, but systemically the organization was as hierarchical as ever.

I was not surprised by the business result after I understood the situation. Senior management, however, was not ready to hear what I had to say. They politely thanked me for the report and decided to increase the training in problem solving.

Collaborative

The feminine collaborative approach involves operating in a coop-erative way. People who use this approach—usually women—generally seek out and enjoy working in a peer-to-peer environment. They share credit with all contributors and focus on getting the job done rather than on taking charge. They listen well, verify their assumptions, and are gen-erally open to others' ideas. While they are willing to share data, power, and themselves, they take personal responsibility for their job, customers, and environment.

One woman manager explained: "I focus on the good things my group has done in management meetings. Others try to take credit for themselves. My approach was viewed as a lack of self-confidence at first, but now I notice that more staff members are doing it the way I do."

Another said, "Women see and hear all sides, they take and use critical input, they are cooperative and don't need to be the captain."

A third manager said, "I don't have to see myself as the only one who makes things work. It's more important that the team makes it work."

People who work collaboratively give credit where credit is due, regardless of an employee's position. They are able to manage a program without authoritarian power by creating a team atmosphere and getting people aligned.

Women who use the collaborative approach are often seen as weak by those who are embedded in the old-style business culture. Those who espouse a "new style of leadership," however, expect more collaboration, as reported by Aburdene and Naisbitt (1992, 98): " 'We have a different style of management than men,' says Denver consultant Jean Yancey. 'And we're seeing we get more productivity if we use it.' Every item on the experts' lists of leadership qualities, she notes, 'openness, trust, ongoing education, compassion and understanding,' describes the female leadership style."

Territorial

The masculine territorial approach is to try to establish power and control over a department or situation as soon as possible in a new appointment. Many men prefer to be in complete control and will fend off incursions aggressively. Many of my interviewees relate the male territorial sense to the fact that men like independent action. They indicate that women seem to have difficulty in accepting this natural and often useful approach.

> Men are more comfortable when they are in command and can dictate the direction.

> Men seem to be much more territorial. That is, they have their own empire and make themselves indispensable. For example, they are less likely to cross-train people or to delegate. They don't seem to worry about who else could do their job in an emergency.

Masculine energy is the energy of command, control, and objectification. It is outgoing, pushing, and invasive. It is natural for masculine energy to create territory for itself and then seek to expand what is already owned.

Men and women each have both masculine and feminine energy—but in different proportions. Some women have learned or acquired an additional proportion of masculine energy to help them in business. Those men who have a high degree of feminine energy tend to suppress it, since it is not valued, especially in business.

Emotional

A greater emotional range is most definitely associated with the feminine approach. The women I interviewed tended to see themselves as having inner emotional strength, able to be vulnerable as appropriate, and able to admit their own mistakes. At the lighter end of the spectrum, they can also be exuberant, excited, or vivacious. In the business setting, women's tendency to cry when they are upset or angry is often strongly associated with "being emotional."

Since "big boys don't cry," men grow up with little skill at dealing with the open expression of emotions—their own or others'. They generally conclude that if someone is crying, something must be terribly wrong, but that is not always the case. Some women (by no means all) cry about minor things. They cry when they are frustrated; they cry when they are touched by a kind deed; they even cry when they are empathizing with the pain of another. In order to be accepted in the workplace, women learn not to cry on the job. The rule against tears is very clear. In the movie *A League of Their Own*, a woman outfielder cries when the male manager of her team criticizes her skills; then, in great frustration, he tells her in no uncertain terms that "there is no crying in baseball." There is also no crying in business.

Crying isn't the only emotional outlet that is shut down at work. Men are allowed to get angry, but not women. In fact, most emotions are frowned upon. The result is that women have to turn off part of themselves from nine to five. Men do too, but many are unaware of this—at least until they hit midlife crisis.

One female senior executive noted, "My natural reaction, that is, my whole emotional range, is not considered appropriate. I have shut down anything that could remotely be interpreted as sexual. This also includes vitality, liveliness, and creativity."

Since women are well attuned to emotions, they are better at admitting mistakes and fear. When someone in a group team admits this type of emotional truth, the whole group is able to move toward more truth. And when a team is truthful, more work gets done with greater ease. The group releases its energy for work rather than tying it up in fear, making excuses, saving face, or trying to work individual agendas. Since women have easier access to emotional truth, they can play a useful role in any group, when it is perceived as safe to do so.

Stoic

The masculine stoic approach is to hide one's feelings. Hiding one's own feelings often accompanies great discomfort with others' emotions. Stoics will go out of their way to avoid any confrontation that has a chance of generating emotions. Men are typically better at setting these kinds of boundaries than women are.

My interviewees report that men communicate in an impersonal style, talking "at arm's length about such thing as sports," as one woman noted.

In particular, men are under great pressure not to admit fear except to a close confidante. It is part of the masculine code to "keep a stiff upper lip," as the British put it. It is an example of the way in which men are limited by the culture to using only a portion of themselves. The women I interviewed made these observations:

> Women admit their fear and are better at expressing and reading it.

> Men don't understand emotion or how to deal with it.

> Men have feelings, they just don't show them.

These comments were made by women after I had asked them to generalize and after they had stated that they knew many who did not fit the generalizations they were about to give me.

> Allison, an executive in a public relations firm, was asked to handle an emotionally charged situation for a client company explicitly because she *was* a woman. A number of people had just been laid off in the client company, and management wanted their consultants to be present at a general meeting following this announcement. The consulting company's president asked Allison to

represent her firm to the employees. She realized that the men were extremely uncomfortable in dealing with this event, which would inevitably generate a great deal of emotion. She did not enjoy having to carry out this duty, but accepted the responsibility because she knew that she would, in fact, be better at presenting the situation and handling its emotional aftermath than the male managers.

Self-Doubting

Self-doubt—a characteristic of the feminine approach—drives women to gather more information than is necessary to support their point. Self-doubters are thorough and careful, but will often nonetheless blame themselves for problems or errors. Self-doubters take criticism personally and may look for authority figures to tell them what to do. Women today are more confident than those of the previous generation, yet self-doubt is still a major challenge to their self-esteem.

There are two aspects to self-doubt: realism and pessimism. Women may be more *realistic* than men about the match between their skills and the goal or position they are trying to achieve. Since women have greater access to their emotions, they are able to be truthful with themselves about their skills and experience. When women are faced with the option of taking on a new challenge, they are more likely than men to cautiously assess their capabilities for success. If they realize they do not have experience or expertise in some area, they will seek out expert advice or look for additional training.

The second aspect of self-doubt is more problematic. Women may be more *pessimistic* than men about the match between their skill and the goal or position they are trying to achieve. Often women back away from a challenge because they doubt their own abilities. They believe they have to know everything about their project or business unit and be able to carry out every task needed to achieve the goal before they can take on an assignment. The following are typical comments made during the interviews:

Women beat themselves up too much.

I analyze too much; I may need to be more of a risk taker.

I have a sense of my place—what decisions I can and can't make.
I'm not sure if that's good or bad.

Women may not give themselves enough credit for their ability to learn as they go.

Confident

The confident masculine approach is to assume one can do any job, achieve any goal. This brings with it a sense of entitlement regarding such issues as promotions and salary. Confident employees—usually men—generally know what they think about any issue and may have trouble seeing a different viewpoint. Most do not take mistakes personally; they do not assume they are incompetent.

A number of women in the study stated that they admire men for assuming they can do anything. Many of the women I interviewed wish they felt as sure of themselves as men do, but they believe that the appearance of confidence in men is often only that—an appearance. Leaders in the business world seem to be required by their system to be, or appear to be, confident. Yet men and women who are overly confident, particularly those who are so self-absorbed that they do not listen to the ideas of others unless they come from someone at a higher level, seem to be using bravado—false confidence—to look as though they fit the leadership mold.

The following are typical of the comments interviewees made about this characteristic:

Men let go of things quicker, while women agonize over the after-leavings.

They [men] don't take their mistakes as seriously or as personally as women do.

Men have a great ability to focus on a task with amazing determination. They have confidence that they will succeed.

Two Different Pictures

There are advantages to both the masculine and feminine approaches to business that can be used effectively if only we can all loosen up and admit we can learn something. Women can learn to use logic, to focus on achieving results, and certainly to be more self-confident. Men can learn to consider more aspects of a situation, to consider the process of how to achieve a goal, and to be more inclusive and more collaborative. There are both women and men who are already incorporating other-gender elements into their working styles. However, there is still a great deal more that can be done by both genders in this regard.

To operate as an integrated person (female or male), it is not sufficient to merely understand that we are all socially predisposed to act in a gender-specific way. To break old patterns, we have to first decide how we would like to react and realize that it is possible to change. Breaking old patterns is the key.

PART TWO

The Five Success Strategies

4

The Emulator

The Emulator is a woman who has reviewed the business opportunities for women and concluded that her most likely route to success lies in behaving as much like a successful businessman as possible. The Emulator usually models her conduct and manner on those of the most aggressive men in the organization because she perceives them as successfully focused on gaining results. Consciously or unconsciously, the Emulator attempts to eliminate or cover up any of her own feminine traits that might be considered weak or soft. She strives to become one of the boys, and often succeeds in becoming more macho than any of them. Competitive and often driven to succeed, she defines success in traditional terms—money, position, power, authority—but does not necessarily believe that a career has to exclude a good family life.

The Emulator is extremely sensitive to the business restrictions imposed upon her as a female: the subtle (and not so subtle) comments about her gender from male colleagues and managers; the exclusion from business discussions that matter; the lack of mentoring by male and female executives; the inability to take a leave of absence to have a family and return to an equal position; the inequality of pay and position; and the threat of sexual harassment. Her clear understanding of the difficulties faced by women in business results in the Emulator's determination not to be a victim. She wants her success to reflect her abilities and is willing to camouflage or eliminate any feminine traits that she thinks might impede her progress.

The Story of One Emulator

Sarah, an investment broker in her mid-forties, was raised in a male-dominated, sports-oriented family. Family activities centered on competition both on and off the playing field. As a middle child with three brothers, Sarah was treated as "one of the boys" and grew up feeling comfortable with men and their interests. She boasted that she never had a dress until she was eight and didn't learn to use makeup until she was thirty-two. Always athletic, she still competed in triathlons whenever she had time.

When Sarah left school, her ambition was to become a stockbroker and make a million dollars. She had a good grounding in business and finance and had held several summer intern jobs as a runner for an investment firm. Upon graduation she landed a full-time job and felt she was on her way up.

Entering the workforce in the early 1970s brought some surprises. It was quickly apparent to Sarah that women's opinions were not considered as valuable as men's, and it was difficult to get a fair hearing for her ideas. Still, she felt that as long as she learned the ropes, she would be able to out perform any of her peers. She was determined to make whatever sacrifices were necessary to achieve her goals. In her zeal, she quickly dismissed any concerns she had that the path she was choosing might be emotionally and personally costly.

Sarah cultivated a direct, no-nonsense working style. She sought situations where she would be required to give tough feedback to reinforce her image of strength to management. She was the one who recommended dropping a block of funds managed by a group of women when their performance took a downturn, even though other brokers said that they had long-term performance potential. When she was out with the men from her office, Sarah could be counted on to laugh at all their dirty jokes and tell a few of her own.

Sarah paid special attention to her boss. She realized he would soon become a partner, and she hoped he would appreciate her talents and move her up with him. One afternoon, just after closing, she and her boss were discussing a difficult client when a peer of hers walked by on her way home. "Have to pick up the kids today," she explained. Sarah's boss looked at her, shook his head, and said, "Well, she's made *her* choice." Sarah agreed with him, adding that their business required long hours and it was certainly a shame that some bright people didn't have the sticking power to do what it took to succeed. Privately, Sarah concluded that if she were ever to have children, she would be sure to have her domestic arrangements airtight.

As Sarah moved up in the organization, she began to see that it would take too long to become a partner to suit her long-term plan. She decided to take a job managing the foreign exchange portfolio for a successful manufacturing firm. There, her extensive knowledge of finance and investing paid off. Four years later, she was named a vice president of the firm, the first woman and the youngest person ever to hold that position.

Although none of Sarah's subordinates or peers liked her, they all agreed that she was smart, made good decisions, and was fair. It was considered prestigious but difficult to work in her organization. At the time, Sarah was only vaguely aware of the feelings of her colleagues.

When Sarah was forty-five she suffered a serious illness that kept her away from work for a considerable time. During her convalescence she discovered two things that shocked her: The first was that her organization seemed to operate perfectly well without her; in fact, morale seemed to have improved. The second was that after the first flurry of flowers and cards, no one from work came to visit her. Only her secretary called her with any regularity. While in the hospital, Sarah spent time thinking over the course of her career. She remembered wondering in the early years about the sacrifices she might have to make to succeed. It saddened her, as she lay in the hospital bed, to realize that support and connection were two important segments of her life that had been left behind.

However, after returning to work, Sarah regained her hard edge. She found several changes she could make in the organization, proving to herself that she was indeed needed. When I asked her how successful she felt, she wondered if she should have done something differently, yet she couldn't imagine what that might be. She quickly shook off any such thoughts as being weak and silly. She felt that she had adapted to an antagonistic environment by being tough and that there was no other course open to her.

Reflections on the Story of Sarah

Sarah is a classic Emulator. Her story illustrates how working in an inhospitable environment can narrow a woman's perceived choices. Competitive women who aspire to high-level jobs seldom know of any successful role models who are not male. Emulators, because of their intense desire to succeed, are drawn to follow those with the highest salaries and greatest authority. Sarah patterned herself after a former CEO who was generally considered to be ruthless but also effective in driving the company forward. Sarah considered him her mentor. There is nothing wrong in learning business skills from men. The problem is that Sarah and other Emulators, by choosing to model themselves on the most aggressive men, leave most of their feminine selves unexplored and undeveloped.

Women who adopt emulation of masculine work styles as a success strategy do so because they feel they have no other choice. There are few successful female models to be found in large companies because, regardless of the ratio of women to men in the workforce, few women make it to the top. Sadly, women who do manage to reach executive levels, regardless of the strategy they use, do not feel free to reach out to younger women to mentor them; and younger ambitious women suspect they will be penalized if they model themselves on the only successful woman in their company. This is pointed out by the research conducted by Ann Morrison and her colleagues for *Breaking the Glass Ceiling* (1992). Executive women, the authors found, generally felt unable to assist younger women, knowing such actions would be detrimental to their image:

> Most of the women we interviewed (61 percent) said they don't try to be a role model. . . . They know that their own success is fragile, and if they fail in their own endeavors, it will hurt other women at least as much as the lack of counsel and support [p. 162].

Strong, successful women do exist in the workforce, but they are generally found running small businesses—companies they started after leaving the large corporate institutions, companies they can run their own way. Read Joline Godfrey's *Our Wildest Dreams* (1992) for an uplifting portrait of such entrepreneurs. These female examples are, of course, not generally visible to the majority of women who work for larger companies. The women who remain in the large corporations and who exhibit a more balanced approach to their work have not reached the upper corporate ranks in sufficient numbers to be able to exert an influence on those following.

One young Emulator, a software engineer, said:

> Work is like a foreign country. It's different than I thought it would be. School seemed more equal. Here it seems more backward. I was surprised that all the top people are male. Their wives are at home, and the men don't seem comfortable with women working. I expected more progress with these men. My approach is to try to use male traits. I try not to be as lively as I really am, and I am careful to dress to look businesslike.

Another, a thirty-eight-year-old program manager in a food conglomerate, said:

> I have a no-nonsense approach—a strict professionalism. This has pretty much eliminated the sexual harassment I experienced

earlier. I like to discuss difficult issues with people one-on-one. One guy tore me down in a meeting, but I confronted him alone afterward. I told him in no uncertain terms never to do that to me again.

I would like to give people more of a chance, but there is a danger in being perceived as weak. I'm watched, so I have less flexibility. I'm male-oriented, so it's easy for me to just fit in.

When women imitate men, the resultant style is somewhat strained. Thus the Emulator is not a true copy of a masculine style. And, it bears repeating, not all men operate in the style Emulators have chosen to imitate. The Emulator feels it is necessary to adopt what she perceives as a successful approach in order to be accepted.

Burdened with an awareness of limited options and with few or no female role models to copy, the Emulator focuses on developing those skills and attributes—some innate, some acquired—that she believes will best serve to advance her career. But in giving all her attention to a narrow range of her personality and talent, she overlooks or buries much of herself and what she has to offer.

Many Emulators are able to ignore symptoms of friction that may point to a lack of self-alignment, especially when they are convinced that their choices are limited by business reality. Sarah has no regrets, at least none of which she is conscious. But many women abandon the Emulator strategy. Their small pangs grow with time, and it is only in looking back that Emulators realize that the direction they have chosen leads them away from themselves—and that that strategy, with its narrow masculinity, causes them discomfort and unhappiness.

Caught up in refining the skills they think are necessary to their success in the business world, Emulators often let years go by before they begin to question their strategy. It is as though they have developed such momentum that they require either a personal crisis or a cutting off of the original energy source to slow them down enough to see what they have missed along the way. The Emulator fears that if she does not sustain this drive with all the force she can muster, she will not achieve her objectives. If the business environment were more receptive to the feminine, Emulators might not feel pushed into overcompensating.

Self-Alignment for the Emulator

Not all Emulators are unhappy with their choice. A woman will change to another role only if she feels dissatisfaction or a desire for something more in her life. However, when we apply the model for alignment (conscious mind, subconscious, and higher self) to the Emulator, we can see why this choice is an uneasy one for some women.

Internally, an Emulator may hear herself making statements such as:

- I'm smart.
- I have lots of skills.
- I have plenty of energy and determination to accomplish all my goals.

The Emulator believes she has good self-esteem; however, she may not be aware of her inner conflicts. She may have doubts about herself of which she is unaware. All former Emulators I interviewed were clear that they began to sense this at some point.

Outwardly, the Emulator often has some good friends and may be in a committed relationship. However, she finds (if she looks) that a number of people at work do not particularly like her. She may believe that "they" are out to get her or that "they" are luckier than she. She is very aware of discrimination and harassment toward women.

The Emulator, then, has some knowledge of her self-talk and belief structures. She is not in communication with her higher self. She is likely to find such a concept silly or a waste of time, since she does not see the connection between it and her ability to succeed.

The Emulator's Approach to Doing Business

The Emulator is determined not to be a career woman who fails simply because she is female. The Emulator tries to play down any suggestion that her femininity makes her less than men or different from men. She adopts a no-nonsense approach, expresses her ambition to move up, and plays all out to win. One woman I interviewed put it this way:

> My style is more masculine. I don't tend to beat around the bush—I'm very direct. I'd share more emotions if it was OK. Overall, my strategy is to play their game. I change myself to fit into their culture. You need to see how people behave and what's important to them, and then you adapt. Men are not trying to make us change. They don't see it as a man's thing—it's just the way it is.

The Emulator, especially in the later stages of her career, often ignores her female colleagues. One female manager complained, "I don't understand why women are particularly hard on other women. You would think that we could support each other better." The business culture makes it difficult for upper-level women to support younger ambitious women. Too much emphasis on women's issues undermines the older women's credibility. This unspoken policy reinforces the limits on the number of women in the higher ranks and makes it difficult for other women to attain those levels.

Emulators are often confused or frustrated by their (usually) unconscious feelings of incongruity. Being out of alignment with their true natures takes a toll, even if they are not aware of it. This internal friction generally leads women who are Emulators to take one of two tracks: they apply themselves even harder to succeed, gradually becoming, like Sarah, caricatures of the hard-nosed businesswoman, or they reach a turning point in self-realization that leads them to move to one of the other success strategies.

Advantages of the Emulator Approach

Ambitious women gain certain advantages by virtue of choosing to be Emulators. Because they are assertive, their skills are noticed sooner than those of other women, and they are often picked early for advancement. The detrimental aspects of the strategy are either not seen early on or are not considered critical. Emulators, in general, are viewed by men as fitting into the business culture. Men find it easier to accept them into the club than to accept women using other success strategies.

It is always a difficult management task to separate out employees with early potential for promotion from the real "keepers"—those who will be groomed and rewarded to ensure they will remain with the organization. Early in a woman's career, it is difficult to see whether she will take on what she perceives to be a successful masculine approach or will eventually develop a balance of skills that might be more effective in the long run.

The business environment encourages Emulators, and being competitive, intelligent people, they are more than happy to respond in the traditional way. It will take longer for more balanced women to develop into "keepers" because business does not yet support self-aligned people who are capable of using a wide range of both masculine and feminine skills.

It is easy for Emulators to ignore early career evaluations that state that their style is too cold, harsh, or even difficult, because they are being rewarded for their behavior by being promoted. Most companies do not consider these traits a major problem until the Emulator has risen to the senior ranks. Management has a tendency to overlook the warning signs that Emulators are on a path that will eventually prove to be self-limiting because Emulators are women who have proven themselves in so many other ways.

> One capable young woman was given a big promotion and at the same time was given feedback from her boss that her peers and her management team found her hard to take. The implication was that she should soften her style. However, her manager's message was delivered in such a way that she never seriously considered the need to make a change. She found it difficult to give much credence to the warning because it came

in the same meeting in which she was told of the promotion. She was so pleased with her move up that she could not hear the criticism.

Many women find that the Emulator approach is useful in heading off sexual harassment. The Emulator's steely demeanor keeps men from approaching her in an unwanted sexual way. One young potential Emulator said, "I am careful to dress in a serious way because the men think I'll be gone soon. At first, people didn't trust me because they thought I'd get married and leave, but they are starting to see me as dedicated to my work and my career."

Another said, "I bury my femininity, but that's easy for me to do. I've always felt like one of the guys. For me it's easy to hang out with them and talk about sports and politics."

Women feel that, as Emulators, they are able to fit in. Being a woman in business automatically brings visibility. For most women, the visibility is more an uncomfortable disadvantage than an advantage, and to cope with the discomfort, they decide that the best strategy is to reduce their visibility by acting like everyone else does, that is, like men do. They worry that being visible as women will mean that they are seen as less capable of serious work or advancement. Being an Emulator is perceived as good camouflage. And in many companies it works well.

Disadvantages of the Emulator Approach

Women who emulate a masculine conversational style are judged differently and more harshly than more feminine women; as Deborah Tannen (1990) notes, such behavior is not considered "acceptable" in a woman. Both women and men are generally uncomfortable with women who swear a lot, tell dirty jokes, or use strong terms to talk about destroying the competition. Such women have crossed a boundary between female and male. We have no category for such individuals and do not know how to deal with them. In fact, we generally prefer not to deal with them at all. We tend to fear those we cannot understand.

EMULATOR CHECKLIST

Advantages	Disadvantages
Early advancement	Stall out later on
Easily accepted	Judged harshly
Visible	May feel something is missing
Protection against sexual harassment	Left out feminine side

Imitating men does not work in the long run, either in terms of a woman's career or in terms of her personal life. One Emulator who eventually changed her style claimed that the most dangerous role for a businesswoman is becoming "one of the boys"; dangerous because

> you give up who you are, and then they can turn on you. You wind up having to denigrate other women to be part of the club. You are just denying your own identity.

Although she climbs quickly to high levels, the Emulator does not generally make it to the most senior levels of management. Macho women are often barred from executive positions. Morrison and her colleagues (1992, 62) found that "being too tough is the kiss of death"—another gender inequality, since harsh and aggressive men often make it to the top.

With a few years' perspective, Emulators who move on to other strategies end up regarding their earlier Emulator role as threatening to their feminine working identities. Unless they remain in the role, women become aware that the part of themselves they eliminated was the feminine side.

The Emulator strategy tends to be used earlier rather than later in a career. It is an excellent way to get started quickly moving up the corporate ladder, and the difficulties that accompany the role usually are not apparent for several years. All the women who spoke of having once used this strategy did so early in their careers and turned to other approaches later on.

Shifting from the Emulator Approach

A number of the women I interviewed told me that they had, at one time in their careers, used the Emulator success strategy and that, in retrospect, they could not believe the way they had acted. One woman said,

> I had become a parody of myself. I can't believe now the things I did then. I certainly was not myself, and I'm much happier now.

Another spoke of her sympathy for herself and other women in this role:

> The way the business culture is, it's no wonder that I acted that way, and I know why others do it, too. You are almost forced into it.

Younger women who have recently entered the workforce are also concerned that they are falling into the old business style. One woman said,

> I don't know if I am losing myself and falling into "their" way of doing things.

Women who are living and working the furthest out of synch with their feminine natures are robbing themselves of their real strength and find it necessary to devise some method to defend themselves against real or imagined attack. They aggressively defend their choices and solutions in order to avoid any conflict within themselves. It is exhausting work.

Those women who do shift away from the Emulator style admit that changing is not easy. Emulators are not likely to move into the Trooper role because it is incompatible with their competitive personalities. Emulators who decide to change strategies generally apply all their intensity to making the change and are successful in their efforts.

Former Emulators become Balancers, Seekers, or Integrators, and generally make great Seekers.

In order to change, Emulators need to develop their softer, relational side. Having learned how to be authoritarian, they must now learn how to be egalitarian; having learned how to tell others what to do, they must learn to trust others to know what to do, given appropriate guidance. When we learn any new skill, it is common to vacillate between the old and the new until we gradually find a balance that works. A transitioning Emulator may, for example, go overboard in allowing people freedom to direct their own activities, then reverse for a period to a more controlling style. Eventually the Emulator will settle into a new style that works as well for her as it does for her peers and subordinates.

> Early in my career I shifted away from the Emulator role as the result of a specific event. I was propelled into this change by attending a personal growth workshop by accident. At that event, I began to see the ways in which I was tight, defensive, and controlling, and I didn't like the information one bit. At the same time, my boss informed me that my clients were unhappy with me. The two discoveries sent me reeling. I had been trying so hard to do the right things at work and to act in ways I thought were correct. I felt betrayed by something or someone, but I couldn't tell what or who. I had put so much energy into my career, and here I was, going in the wrong direction. Since I wasn't sure what was right anymore, I felt I had to change everything. I cut my hair, bought clothes in a more casual style, divorced my husband, gave up singing, took up hiking, changed my personality, and changed careers. I was way up there on the stress curve.
>
> I was an information systems (IS) manager at the time, and the workshop revealed to me the whole field of organization development (OD), a discipline devoted to structuring organizations to accomplish their goals while at the same time changing the culture

to reflect a more humanistic approach to using the potential of individual employees. I was drawn to the practitioners of this work because they seemed to have a clearer understanding of themselves and others. I understood neither and decided to make a career change. My manager was bewildered but supportive.

I was already working on an M.B.A. degree and decided to add a concentration in OD. Through that area of study I learned a great deal about the theory of organizations and their ability and inability to change. At the same time, I attended workshops on topics as varied as "Centering" and "Theory and Practice of Training," for a more experiential view of my chosen field. I also learned several of the techniques of team building and practiced them on the group I managed. I got a job as an OD consultant and, at first, didn't have a clue as to what exactly I ought to do. For a while, my performance ratings suffered, and my pride with them. At the same time, I realized that my life was moving in a positive direction and I had taken a giant step toward being myself.

The Key Issue for Emulators

Women in many companies are finding that they are no longer the object of comments about their figures or female behavior; their male colleagues are now polite, even helpful. On the other hand, the same women are still not being assigned to the better projects they need for advancement, nor are they given adequate information about their performance. The ideas women contribute are still often ignored. Many men believe that the problems have disappeared and are bewildered when they hear women complain. "It was easier to deal with [discrimination] in the old days, when it was overt," moaned one female manager.

Covert discrimination exists in many companies. Even when management supports programs for equal opportunity and valuing diversity, change is extremely slow in coming. Highly competitive and ambitious women prefer taking on the direct challenge of their careers to wrangling with the indirect hurdles of sexism. Many find that the way around the hurdles is to become an Emulator. Emulators find it difficult to see how they could function successfully in the business world in any other way. However, many Emulators eventually tire of wearing a masculine mask to make their careers work. They discover that they have locked away their feminine face and realize that they want to let that whole woman out again.

There is a difference between wanting to succeed (most career women do) and acting in the traditional (masculine) ways. Women want to achieve whatever their capabilities will allow and want the satisfaction of meeting challenges and accomplishing their goals. As such, they are competitive. For Emulators, the real challenge is learning how to successfully pursue career goals, using what they have learned about masculine behavior, while incorporating more of their feminine nature and abilities into their total style and acting in a congruent way.

5

The Trooper

The Trooper tries as best she can to anticipate and provide whatever is—or might be—needed by her manager and her peers. Her primary strategy is to work hard, and she focuses on competency rather than on office politics. Careful to be prepared for every meeting, the Trooper will amass enormous amounts of data to support any point she might want to make. She often feels exhausted or burned out because of the sheer amount of work she has taken on. Motivated by a need for approval, she tries to get along with everyone and is usually well liked by people at all levels of the organization. Though the Trooper role can produce some traditional success, this strategy is the least likely of the five to lead to a senior or executive management role because the Trooper is too busy with minor chores to take strategic action. The Trooper may be too overworked to take much satisfaction from her job and tend to rely on aspects of her private life for her feelings of fulfillment.

The Story of a Trooper

Working under a senior marketing manager, Joan was a midlevel manager for an automotive manufacturer. Her group was responsible for providing the promotional materials for one of the top American car lines. Joan was a tall woman who carried her considerable weight well. She dressed in a subdued but stylish manner.

Even though she had reached a reasonably high level, Joan did not feel particularly successful. She realized that she would get no higher in her career. Now in her mid-fifties, she was considering early retirement, but feared that she would be bored because her children had already left home.

> What will I do with myself? The kids don't need much from me except for some babysitting and a shoulder to cry on from time to time. I can't just sit at home reading women's magazines and trying new recipes for low-fat meals. At the same time, I am tired of the struggle at work; every day is the same and I don't know how much longer I can stand it.

Joan married immediately after she graduated from college in 1962, but her husband did not make much money so they postponed having a family and decided she should get a job. She had a degree in English and enjoyed reading and writing so she found work as an assistant to a newspaper columnist. Joan was aware that she was a bit out of step with her sixties contemporaries who were either getting involved with the counter-culture or having children. But she did not think of herself as having a career. She only expected to work until starting her family.

Nevertheless, Joan did want to do a good job and so she applied herself to her work just as she had at college. Since her approach to school had resulted in good grades, Joan reasoned that it might also result in approval at work. While in school, she had managed to squeeze in fifty-two hours of study time a week outside of classes. Only in retrospect did Joan think that might have been excessive. However, she applied the same strategy to her job, working long hours and carefully researching everything she was given to do. It was a point of pride with her that she went into every meeting completely prepared. She willingly helped on any project and was often still in the office after seven, even on Friday night.

Joan saw her long hours paying off in experience and responsibility. When her husband moved to Chicago to take another job, his new company offered her a position as well, in the marketing department. The couple was delighted with this package and settled down in a suburb, intent upon setting enough money aside to allow Joan to take some time off to start the family her mother-in-law had been hinting about for some time.

When Joan did get pregnant, she found it a definite disadvantage at work. Her manager would pat her stomach and call her "little mother." She was enraged at his condescending attitude but did not dare complain for fear of antagonizing him. She decided to stop working in favor of full-time motherhood.

After two children, Joan realized that she liked working and the additional income it provided. Her sister-in-law happily agreed to care for the children when Joan returned to a job with her old Chicago company (loyalty is another of Joan's qualities). She soon realized that she had lost time—people much younger had passed on to higher levels—and she felt "behind the eight ball." Leaving work in time to put the children to bed made her look less devoted than other employees.

Joan relied once again on her ability to research and work hard to win her manager's approval. Every marketing piece was accompanied by a large stack of folders with research to support every point. She learned more about the properties of vinyl than most plastic experts. Although most of her preparation was never used or questioned, Joan was proud of the fact that she always had the facts right and could support her manager. She found that people trusted her work and she liked that feeling, but it never translated into the kind of promotions she thought her work deserved.

Today, Joan is still frustrated about what it takes to get ahead. She says she thinks things out fully before coming to a decision and likes to develop her subordinates. She is also implementation-oriented and able to get things accomplished. With her skills obvious, she does not understand why she is not more recognized and valued. "The male managers don't seem to do any of these things, yet they get the raises and promotions while I am overlooked," she said in a bewildered voice. Joan's job included promoting a line of cars geared to the woman buyer, and yet her ideas about what women want in a car have been discounted and diminished. By choice, she did not engage in office politics, but stated that she still did not understand why her opinion as a woman is not sought out more.

According to Joan, competence was the key to the partial success she had attained, and she believes that working harder and doing good enough work will eventually earn her the recognition she seeks. However, she acknowledges that this approach has not really been working for her and is at a loss as to what her next move should be.

Reflections on the Story of Joan

Joan's story demonstrates a problem that plagues many working women: Even though they recognize that hard work is only part of the equation for success, they have a difficult time identifying the missing pieces. Because the Trooper believes that hard work *should* be rewarded, she assumes that the lack of raises and promotions means she has not worked hard enough. At the same time, the Trooper may be concerned that she will be reprimanded or even fired if she does not accomplish everything asked of her. "Work equals reward" falls into the same old-fashioned, black-and-white belief system as "sin equals punishment." Since there is an almost theological underpinning to her belief, the Trooper is uncomfortable with the idea of dismantling it even when it becomes apparent that it does not work. This simple equation must be right because, in her mind, the alternatives would lead to anarchy.

But raises and promotions are not the only rewards at stake. Troopers want to do a good job. They are loyal to their company and try their best to contribute to its success.

One loyal young Trooper told me about her experience when she returned from taking a maternity leave. The company gave her a job comparable to the one she had been doing, but soon after her return, the man who had taken her old job left. Her boss asked her to do both jobs since she knew the department so well. In addition, he piled on some other duties so she was effectively being asked to do two and a half jobs, for the same salary. This Trooper valiantly tried to figure out how to accomplish all this work and was convinced that if she refused any portion of it, she would be reprimanded or fired.

The Trooper exemplifies the tendency of many women to emphasize competence over confidence. Success in business requires both. In the current business environment, making sure that others know what you have done is as important as doing it. Accomplishing the task shows competence and announcing responsibility for the job and the results shows confidence. There are women who use all five success strategies who lack the self-esteem to tell their bosses or managers about their accomplishments, but low visibility is especially prevalent among Troopers.

Figure 5.1. Competence-Confidence Relationship.

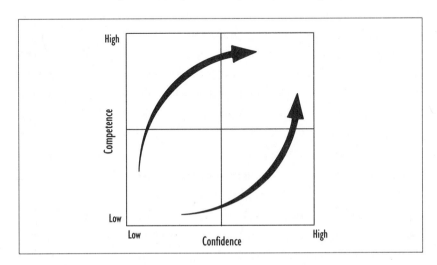

Figure 5.1 illustrates the relationship between confidence and competence. Any skill you have or want to acquire—say, the ability to give good presentations—can be evaluated in these terms. I generally call the lower arrow the "fake it till you make it" route. The upper arrow indicates the route often, but not exclusively, taken by Troopers. (In general, more women than men use it.) Getting past the upper left quadrant is a special problem for Troopers, who tend to migrate to the upper left-hand quadrant, where competence is high and confidence is low.

When learning a new skill or when dealing with a skill in which they have no interest, most people start out in the lower left quadrant, with low confidence and low competence. I have both low confidence and low competence with regard to newspaper layout, internal medicine, and bungee jumping, and I don't want or expect to change quadrants for any of them. However, I also see my poetry writing skill in this quadrant, but wish to advance to the upper right quadrant—high confidence and high competence—with respect to this skill.

The upper right quadrant represents both skill mastery and an awareness and expression of that mastery; it is the desired state with regard to the skills we require at work each day. Women and men tend to move toward this quadrant in different ways. Men generally move first to high confidence and low competence and from there to the upper right quadrant—the "just do it" route.

Many women, and especially Troopers, are uncomfortable with this approach. Women tend to develop confidence through knowledge and experience. For them, the route is through high competence and low confidence. When they feel as though they know enough about a topic or have practiced a skill long enough, they begin to feel confidence. For Troopers, crossing the line from low to high confidence is difficult. And one mistake or negative comment about their performance is enough to push them back into low confidence again.

Sometimes Troopers push themselves into slipping back. Self-confidence suddenly seems arrogant, pushy, or conceited to the Trooper. Many feel as though they have set themselves above others. The feeling of equality—even if that means ignoring, suppressing, or denying her skills or strength and slipping back into the upper left quadrant—is more comfortable for the Trooper and makes it difficult for her to express her confidence. Here are some observations from women I interviewed:

> I tend to focus on competency—get really good, get lots of degrees, work hard. That's my approach, in contrast to using lots of influence and playing the political game. I can see this might be a detriment. I might have gotten better positions, but I go for interesting work rather than for the money.

> I only worked on this issue twice. Once I bargained for a promotion by saving a project in trouble. But in general, I keep working harder to prove my worth. I felt that if I did good work, I would be recognized, but I've noticed this doesn't really work.

Hard work and attention to detail do help Troopers rise in their organizations, but Troopers do not generally make it to the highest senior-level positions unless they are able to learn to delegate the detail work and take a more strategic view of their business. Moving into a Balancer mode increases their chances for promotion.

Self-Alignment for the Trooper

The Trooper has fairly good communication between her conscious mind and her subconscious. She is closer to her higher self than the Emulator. One woman wrote,

> Frankly, I feel a lot of affection for the Trooper. While she misses some important points about the business world, I think she is far more aligned with herself than the Emulator.

The self-talk of the Trooper is a mix of the superficial level of internal dialogue and her contradictory beliefs about herself. She may hear herself say:

- I'm smart, but that doesn't seem to be enough.

- I have to learn more.
- I'm really tired, but at least I have my family and friends.
- There seems to be something missing in my ability to be successful.

Thus, she is close to her subconscious, although she may only occasionally hear it.

The Trooper generally has many good friends, and most people like her. She finds that while some people appreciate how hard she works, others give her advice to take better care of herself. She is often frustrated by the fact that some of "them" seem to get ahead on their looks or speech or gender.

The prime motivation for the Trooper is a desire to be liked and respected. She is generally oriented to the outside world for evidence as to whether she has done the right things.

The Trooper's Approach to Doing Business

The Trooper tends to be busy outside of work, devoting time to her family, friends, and other interests. The Trooper often looks to other interests for real satisfaction. When she considers the whole picture, she generally sees her life as productive and satisfying. She may feel frustrated and beaten down by the system at work, but she is nervous at the thought of operating in a more strategic way that would give her more visibility and a shot at more responsibility. Shying away from politics, she may undermine herself when trying to tell others about her accomplishments. For example, she does not come across as strongly as she might or she inadvertently leaves out critical information. A group leader in a manufacturer of large equipment parts said,

> My approach is to build strong teams. To be successful is to get your ideas adopted. I use the team. I get them to help me sell it. I often let others take the credit. I've been a "king-maker"—made my boss look good by passing ideas on to him. This has both good and bad sides. I've avoided political means to get ahead by choice, so I've worked very hard.

Joan expressed confusion and frustration at the way her career was unfolding. The way she saw it, others were promoted just because of their ability to play the politics. She did not understand that those pro-motions might be due to the employees' ability to take risks, forsee the long-term results, or persuade and inspire others—in short, to lead organizations.

The Trooper defines achievement as accomplishing tasks, not leading others. In fact, Joan believed that there was something wrong with her organization because those who rose to leadership did not know how to actually *do* anything, and in her book that is not just. While the Trooper is very much concerned with justice, she may be in denial about her own situation and about the very real barriers women encounter in business. She may even believe that claims of discrimina-tion or harassment are exaggerations. One forty-year-old Trooper I interviewed stated,

> I have never really seen discrimination against women. I don't
> see why women can't be as successful as they want. You just have
> to learn how to act, like applying yourself and not breaking into
> tears.

Success for the Trooper is defined by hard work, job contentment, and winning the fight against negative thinking. When asked about her biggest challenge, one African-American Trooper answered, "You mean besides sexism and racism?" She said that her biggest challenge was to remain positive and find outside interests to keep up her spirits. Accomplishments had come easily to her, while keeping a good atti-tude had been more difficult. Her experiences echoed my own in this respect.

> After I had shifted away from the Emulator approach because of
> the enormous stress in my life, I slipped into the Trooper category.
> I had been wounded by my experience as an Emulator and hoped
> that by keeping out of company politics and working hard, I would
> succeed.

I was recruited into a small consulting group chartered to develop an organization development–based method to change information systems, a natural fit with my background. As a group, we developed and tested a process for integrating IS change with organizational change. This subject had long interested me, and the work added to my earlier experience as an IS manager (I had organized a customer steering committee to oversee the development of a system). I felt challenged by the task and was convinced I was making a significant contribution.

The manager of the group was a visionary, the type who had many grand ideas. He soon got bored and left for another position. Since I had experience, I was asked to manage the group and told to report to a different man who had no understanding of what we had been trying to accomplish. Instead of a visibility problem, our group now had a credibility problem. One by one, the members of the group left, but I kept plugging on. I, too, almost lost hope, and applied to my new boss for a position as a strategic planner. In one of the most devastating meetings of my career, he informed me that he had no confidence that I could do the strategic planning job and no confidence in what I had been doing. He suggested I go back to IS management or find another home for my, by now, singular pursuit. He offered no help with either of these options.

I went home and suffered through one of the worst migraines of my life. When I recovered, something had changed. I decided that he was not going to destroy my new vision and that I was going to rise above this setback. I realized that I needed to take control of my career and my life and that my self-esteem was dragging. I returned to the task of personal growth and was surprised at how easily I found a manager in another part of the organization who was very excited about the prospects of the work I had undertaken. I found a supportive home in her group for the next several years.

TROOPER CHECKLIST

Advantages	Disadvantages
Can succeed	Not likely to get to the top
Liked by all	Often exhausted
Feels proud about doing the right things	May feel they are missing out
	May not feel recognized
Can focus on family	

Advantages of the Trooper Approach

There are some Troopers who have found traditional success. One is a professor of economics and a consultant. Another owns a small automotive parts distributorship with two male partners, one her husband. A third manages a product development department in the computer business. Not all Troopers want to ascend to the highest positions, but there are some who do, even with their limiting strategy of ignoring company politics and working hard.

Many Troopers work primarily to provide the basics for their families. Others work because they want to send their children to college or have nice clothes. Their motivation in working is to do the best job they can in order to bring home a paycheck. They may not think of themselves as having a career, only as having a job. They may have little interest in climbing the corporate ladder.

The Trooper's strategy lets her thrive in the business world while enabling her to provide the quality of personal life she desires.

Disadvantages of the Trooper Approach

The main disadvantage of being a Trooper is exhaustion without satisfaction. Troopers put in eight (and usually more) working hours a day that provide little fulfillment. The overattention to detail and lack of involvement in the larger business picture distance Troopers from the work they really love. In the process, they wind up separated from themselves and are not completely self-expressed.

One Trooper told me how discouraged she has become about her job because she just cannot seem to fit in. She works with a governmental agency concerned with medical care for the aged, and while she loves the idea of her job and wants to contribute to easing the last years of people's lives, she confesses that "I can't seem to get very excited about my work because the political system gets in my way." She does not know what she can do to ease this distress in her work life.

Troopers have trouble finding alternative approaches to their work. The options they do see strike them as even more disagreeable than their present mode. They disapprove of being more assertive and taking charge of their careers because they believe that advancement should come in the form of a reward.

I recently led a workshop for women during which I presented the five success strategies. One participant, a Trooper, told a story I found most interesting. She managed a publications production group responsible for design, layout, and typesetting. She recalled with indignation that she had recently discovered that her senior management believed her group was still using typewriters. She was upset, because the group had been using computers for twelve years. When I commented that perhaps she ought to tell management more about her group, she agreed, but it was clear that she believed in her heart that they ought to have noticed without her having to draw it to their attention. On hearing this story, other Troopers in the room expressed similar feelings. They deplored those who sang their own praises and, by implication, supported the woman who had not done so.

The Key Issue for Troopers

For most Troopers, the only way out of their exhausting life style is to break their own rules. And Troopers, more than any other group, firmly believe in observing the letter of the law—that is, doing things the right way, at least according to their own definition. For these women, expressing confidence by announcing their accomplishments is itself breaking a rule—and also the reason they so easily fall over the low confidence line time and again.

Telling a boss about an accomplishment may not feel right, but it is the accepted way of gaining deserved recognition in our business culture. More important, announcing an accomplishment is a compelling way to express competence and confidence, not just as a businessperson, but as a woman.

Most Troopers feel as though they are bound by a contract to act in limiting ways. They may see that they ought to inform management of their accomplishments, or be more assertive about excessive demands on their time, or promote their unique business talents, but their imaginary contracts with themselves prevent them from taking any of these steps.

Troopers who want to change to other success strategies have to find their self-esteem and learn to express their confidence. While they will probably need to be ever-vigilant regarding their tendency to slip back over the line into low confidence, they can also use this awareness to challenge themselves. Their ability to apply themselves to a task is a considerable advantage. Troopers are the most consistent workers when they have taken on the task of achieving their own self-alignment.

6

The Balancer

The Balancer consciously strives for an equilibrium between the disparate aspects of her life—between her work life and home life, and between her feminine and masculine skills and attributes. Some women find they have to choose between these two life aspects because they cannot find a good mix. One woman described it as being pulled apart by two teams of horses. Many women, however, work hard to find ways of maintaining the right balance (right for them).

The Balancer is ambitious and thinks of herself as a career woman, but one who is also devoted to her family or other outside interests. She understands what is important to the company and focuses her efforts to provide that. When she identifies a problem, she usually has a solution at hand. She knows when and how to make decisions and can take control of a situation. She offers direction to her team or group and gets buy-in from her management.

The Balancer is savvy enough to inform her manager of her progress, especially of any successes she has brought about. Aware that women are expected to be nonassertive, she also realizes that passivity will not produce the results she wants. Even if she dislikes it, the Balancer has learned to play the game well enough to be perceived as successful.

In addition to the masculine skills she cultivates, the Balancer also has access to many feminine attributes. She encourages good teamwork and collaboration and is aware of what it takes to help a team achieve maturity and accomplish its goal. She is also likely to emphasize team success over personal success. To see this balance in action, let us look at the story of a Balancer named Emily.

The Story of a Balancer

Emily is the director of Human Resources for a national hotel chain. She stands a slim six feet tall. She has a narrow face. Her light brown hair is naturally curly and she wears it cut at shoulder length. She has responsibility for setting and evaluating policies for recruitment, compensation, and training. She believes that she should also have responsibility for organizational development and argues that separating it from training lessens the impact of both. The current director of Organization Development has been a friend of the CEO since they were in the military together.

Emily had a difficult first marriage and took some time off after divorcing to recover from that experience. She wanted to provide a good life for her two children and to protect them from the influence of her abusive former husband. She decided to go to law school because she thought it would prevent her from being manipulated by a system that she did not understand and she needed to be able to make a good enough salary to care for her two sons.

After graduating with honors she worked for a law firm for several years. She was intelligent and had a great deal to offer, but she found the situation difficult because it seemed that the only way to succeed was to be competitive, aggressive, and hard. Emily learned a good deal in the law firm environment, but it never seemed to really suit her, so she took a job in the legal department of a manufacturing firm. There her natural tendencies for treating people kindly won more approval and she began to develop the style with which she manages today. She began to learn to balance the hard, confrontive, driving style she had absorbed early in her career and the softer style that encourages people to collaborate, present their ideas, and take responsibility for their own successes and failures. Her style was the reason she was hired away from legal into the personnel department, and there she easily gained several promotions.

Emily felt quite successful even though she realized that she was unlikely to wrest OD from her colleague's control and equally unlikely to rise any higher in the company. She knew that one reason she had risen to director level was because human resources departments are traditionally run by women. She had been told that she was doing an excellent job but that she was not seen as one who was ready for a more strategic role. This was frustrating, since she had been unable to find out what more was expected of her before she would be ready to lead a profit-making division.

Emily was proud of the contribution she had made to the company and believed she had had a part in increasing its market share. She had consistently focused on customer satisfaction and that emphasis had been effective. Customer comments were more positive than before and the increased market share was principally due to an improved rate of return business. She was equally proud of the way her children were growing into mature, responsible young people.

Emily's work style was admired throughout the company. She was even featured in a local newspaper as an example of "feminine leadership." She found the whole exercise amusing because she was just doing what seems reasonable and she knew many men who operated in the same fashion she did. Of course, she was aware that many men and some women were still caught up in a traditional autocratic, hierarchical mode of operating. She hoped that she was having some influence on changing her corporate culture in this regard.

Emily had spent time honing her management skills and finding a way to treat people that was reasonable and effective. Beyond that, she had never before been particularly introspective. Emily was satisfied with the mixture of work and raising her children she had achieved. She had several friends with whom she spent time and expressed no desire to find another mate. She said that managing is like dealing with kids: "You don't really have any power over them, so you have to convince, give ideas, let them experiment, and have them come to you. You have to give up the idea of controlling things and provide advice, counsel, overall direction, boundaries, and a little love."

Emily described her approach to work as competitive, assertive, internally driven, and backed by a strong work ethic. She brought a lot of energy to her job and liked helping people find their own styles. She strongly believed that people want to do a good job and that her role was to help them accomplish that. She had emphatically supported promoting other women even though her male co-workers made feminist jokes at her expense.

Recently Emily found herself wondering if she should be doing something differently. Her sons had left home; one was in graduate school and the other had started a career and married. Emily kept having feelings of discontent but was not sure if they were about her career or some other aspect of her life. The annoyance she felt about her prospects for promotion did not seem to account for this overall sense of wanting something more in her life. "I just don't seem to be successful in finding out who I am," she said to me. She agreed that she certainly was successful in the business aspects of her life. "I think I'll use up my accumulated leave to go to Australia and then New Zealand," she offered. "Maybe the novelty will give me another perspective on life—maybe that's all I need." I didn't think she believed that, but she had no idea what else to do.

Reflections on the Story of Emily

Utilizing both feminine and masculine strategies comes naturally to the Balancer. Many Balancers are, like Emily, acutely aware of being women and of using their "feminine skills," but they find that they have to hide what they are doing by disguising it in masculine terminology.

One Balancer I interviewed, who was a manager, explained how she cited "experts" on the topic of empowerment to defend her actions when her boss asked why she had not confronted an employee about never signing the location log. Her boss was concerned that the young man was doing personal errands on company time. The Balancer knew her employee was creative and hard-working but that he did not respond well to company rules, which he perceived as restricting his freedom. She would have confronted him if he had not been doing his job, but in fact he was a top performer. She felt it was in the best interests of the company to allow him a certain liberty. Since her boss would not take her word for it, she gave him a few books on participative leadership and empowerment. He read them and backed off.

The balanced style can work well for both male and female managers. It is now being adopted by many men, especially younger ones. One man I interviewed described a management style similar to Emily's. He said he had changed in the past few years and his softer style makes it safer for his managers to speak up and contribute their ideas. Making your numbers, he strongly believes, comes from caring about employees and customers. He said he had learned a lot about this from working with strong women managers. On balance, he likes working with women better than working with men only:

> I've loosened up more and that makes it safer for my managers. We went through a reduction in the workforce. The women were more positive and identified their self-worth less on their work than the men did. They had a better center about what's real.
>
> I like working with women. It's a better environment for me. I like to receive more nurturing and also like to provide it.

That women who are Balancers are being emulated by men is surely a good sign for the future. But being a Balancer may not be a perfect solution for everyone. Women who are Balancers are still subject to the general perception that they lack the necessary strength to tackle the truly important jobs.

One young Balancer, an M.B.A. in a managerial job, told me a story about needing some marketing data entered into a database for a major presentation to the Board of Directors. She and her boss went to the data entry department to get the job prioritized. She bent down in order to speak at eye level to the clerk who was sitting at a terminal. She asked for the job to be done right away and explained why. The clerk agreed and immediately started on the project. Her boss berated her, both for bending down and for asking instead of telling. She reminded him that she had gotten cooperation without any resistance, but he continued to disagree with her approach. It was frustrating to her that her style obviously worked, yet her boss remained convinced she ought to use his. This feeling of confusion may lead some Balancers, like Emily, to wonder if something is wrong or if they just need a vacation. This vague sense of discontent can go on for years, with the Balancer feeling that her life is fine in most respects and wondering why she wishes for something more. For those who persist in exploring these feelings, the answer will generally lead to a quest for greater self-alignment, since what is missing is the whole self, not a vacation, a different job, a baby, a new lover, or any of the myriad things we generally think will relieve this longing.

Balancers may at times confuse their colleagues with their combination of drive and vulnerability. Men, they say, don't seem to know how to react to them when they are strong and competitive one moment and empathetic and connective the next.

Balancers can also confuse themselves. They sometimes wonder if they are acting a part or truly being themselves. They find themselves, at times, being too aggressive and have to stop, back up, and retrench. At other times, they find that they are too nurturing or empathetic. One Balancer said that she had learned the hard way, by being fired, that she had to pay more attention to politics. She has asked her current employer to postpone a promotion that would mean a transfer so that she can pursue a personal relationship to see if it will work out. Many women still find they have to choose between family life and work life, a hard decision for anyone to make.

Balancing Work Life and Home Life

The story of Emily does not address the work life/home life balance, yet this topic is of considerable importance and difficulty for many women. Balancers are particularly involved with the issue.

A number of companies have implemented programs to address varied family-centered needs of employees. One woman told of her company's task force on family issues. In addition to offering personal support, the company has set up a child care facility. Employees are allowed to use the facility twenty days a year for free, which is particularly helpful when regular day care arrangements fail. This firm is exemplary in this regard.

Yet even when such programs are available, many who are eligible to use them hesitate to do so. Why? Sue Cornwall, consultant and lecturer on such issues, addressed this question at the Work and Life Conference in Boston in April 1993:

> The answer lies in the very nature of the organization itself—in how it operates, in how things get done—namely, in the culture of the organization. These programs are not used because the organization's culture does not support it. Employees fear that using these benefits means career suicide.

Cornwall gave two examples of individuals who had crossed these cultural norms:

- A [male] computer executive, a seventeen-year employee, who had accumulated vacation time, was criticized as being uncommitted for taking a six-week camping trip with his family.

- A manager in a computer software firm chose to work part-time after her daughter was born. She soon discovered she was not being informed about staff meetings. Upon inquiring why, she was told, "We didn't think you'd care about them, now that you only work part time." Both her co-workers and her boss had decided her commitment to the job and the organization had lessened.

In a personal conversation, Cornwall went on to say that the strictures against female employees are far greater than against males.

It is not easy to keep home and work balanced. Women are still often considered responsible for the family life, and if they can manage a career as well, so much the better for the family finances.

The Balancer's Worldview

Many Balancers have grown up with brothers or with a strong father figure and have dealt with the women's reality of "a man's world" much of their lives. Used to dealing with men, they enter the workforce with an expectation of success. They take a no-nonsense view of work and of the discrimination that women face. They're both realistic and frustrated about being treated as second-class citizens, but most do not allow themselves to become obsessed by anger. They understand the historical source of such treatment and do their jobs as best they can while trying to change the corporate culture.

While purposefully cultivating an assortment of masculine skills, the Balancer also relies unselfconsciously on her natural feminine talents. Her awareness allows her to see the whole picture, and she consciously absorbs all the available data, including the feelings of any people involved. She is aware of using her intuition but knows how to explain her results while remaining vulnerable and able to admit mistakes. The Balancer generously shares both power and success with members of her team, group, or department, and works to develop her subordinates. Recognizing her colleagues for their efforts comes naturally to her. Her nurturing side allows her to care openly about her customers as well as her employees. One of the women I interviewed put it this way:

> I am able to manage a program without authoritarian power. I can create an atmosphere of teamwork. I seem to be out of synch as to when and how I react to pressure. It seems everyone believes in crisis management, but I don't work that way.
>
> I have been accused of putting my family first. Of course I do; there are real lives at stake here. I don't take the business world as seriously as men seem to want to. I've had arguments with management on this.

Perhaps because they have developed a style that suits them and because they give a high level of time and attention to their home lives, most Balancers are not generally concerned about looking further into personal development. Such women may feel they do not have any time to devote to anything else in their lives. Since they are generally satisfied with their balance, they have no particular motivation to seek further. Some find themselves continually trying to decide which aspect of their lives should receive their focus. They may be so stressed with this push and pull that they have no energy to look for other ways to achieve balance.

Self-Alignment for the Balancer

The Balancer has a good measure of overlap between her conscious mind and her subconscious and is somewhat in touch with her higher self. Her self-talk indicates that she is quite satisfied with herself both in terms of how she feels about herself as a person and how well she is doing in her career. She hears herself say:

- I'm pleased with my success.
- My style suits me even though I see I won't make it much higher.
- I wonder if I'm giving enough time to my job/family/friends.
- I wonder if there isn't more to life.

The Balancer has good relationships with people at all levels of work and finds that her subordinates like, trust, and respect her. She is motivated by wanting to feel equally successful at work and in the rest of her life.

Except for the Integrator, the Balancer comes the closest to achieving material success and feeling satisfied with herself. Her individual purpose may be represented by such statements as "I want to feel equally successful at work and in the rest of my life" or "I want to achieve the highest level I can at work and do it with integrity."

The difference between the Integrator and the Balancer is directly related to their levels of self-alignment. Many people live their lives without ever being aware of that difference. They are productive and happy. Others, after living the Balancer life for a time, start to wonder if there isn't more to life. Not that they need more, but they want more. This question will propel them into the Seeker role, a qualitatively different territory.

Advantages of the Balancer Approach

The Balancers that I met and interviewed were clustered in the middle-management ranks, with a few at the vice president and director levels, indicating that the style is generally a successful one. The Balancer strategy is often described as the "feminine leadership" approach.

Balancers report a sense of satisfaction with their capability and effectiveness in the business world. They generally feel that they can fit in with the culture and that they receive adequate recognition from the establishment, yet are able to express themselves as women.

Because of their ability to relate to both male and female work strategies, Balancers can and do influence the business culture. Gary Powell, in *Women and Men in Management* (1988, 130–131), reports, "in some situations, gender stereotyping diminishes without any managerial action required. This happens when workers gain experience over time in working with opposite-sex peers."

BALANCER CHECKLIST

Advantages	Disadvantages
Can be very successful	Still hit the glass ceiling
Liked by most	May feel torn between work
Feel satisfied, capable,	life and home life
and effective	May still feel something is
Can influence the business	missing
culture	

Disadvantages of the Balancer Approach

Balancers who feel divided between their work and home lives are prone to regretting their inability to live up to their career potential. Those with children find it particularly difficult to meet all the demands on their time. They have knowingly sacrificed a higher level of success in order to keep the balance in their lives. Yet, overall, they feel they are doing the best they can with the choices they have made. The more fortunate ones are able to afford excellent child care that relieves them of worry. One woman I interviewed lives with her mother, who cares for the children; another has a husband who stays home by choice; others have hired caregivers who are particularly nurturing.

There are also Balancers who sense that their blending of masculine and feminine strategies is forced, not natural. As they mold themselves to adapt, they begin to lose a sense of themselves in some inexplicable way. One Balancer asked me how she would know if she were being herself or if she were becoming "one of them." Balancers agree that it is very difficult to find and maintain a workable balance.

Balancers may drop out of the traditional workforce, because they are continually seeking better ways to achieve balance in their lives. They may pause in midcareer to reassess, recover their energy, or train for a different career better suited to their need to balance their feminine and masculine energies. When they pause or drop out, they join the ranks of the Seekers, either temporarily or permanently.

I interviewed several Balancers who had made the choice to switch careers. One had left her position as vice president and director of a substantial organization and is now in the process of training for a dual career in hands-on healing and counseling. She is sure now that she prefers to work with individuals and feels a strong urge to express herself in a way that her previous work did not allow, yet she worries that she has "quit" or "given up," pejorative terms she sometimes applies to her actions. She does not like the feeling that she left a career when there was more she could have done.

The Key Issue for Balancers

The description of the Balancer may sound as though it is the best of all possible worlds—and it is the most successful and effective of the success strategies presented thus far. Many women are perfectly satisfied with achieving a balance in their lives and wish for no more. Yet I found many Balancers expressing a desire for something more or something different or something refreshing.

Balancers have difficulty defining the source of their discontent. Some pin it on their work situation and think the solution is to "get out of a big company" or to "get out of a small company" or to "find a non-threatening environment" or to "try to do things the way I want to do them." A Balancer may blame herself for her malaise and believe she needs to "raise my self-confidence" or "let go of my fear and realize how valuable I am." One said simply, "I'm tired of feeling there's something wrong with me."

All of these quotes are from women who have achieved career success and whose life styles are the envy of many.

Identifying the Balancer's angst as an external case of discrimination or as an internal issue of low self-confidence are obvious reactions. It is easy for most women to perceive job discrimination and its impact on self-esteem. However, acknowledging the obvious may obscure the real issue, which is the lack of alignment with the self. It is the urge to express themselves more fully that is at the heart of the discontent experienced by Balancers who want "more."

In the next two chapters I will describe the Seeker and the Integrator. These two strategies are different than the first three. They are employed by women who consciously attempt to find the source of their feelings of discontent by looking within for the answers. They apply the results of that process to their approach to work.

7

The Seeker

The Seeker is a woman who is disturbed by the incongruity she perceives between who she is and what she thinks the working world would like her to be. She is intentionally seeking a way to become whole—to access her natural self—to increase authenticity.

The Seeker's search might mean a period of retreat from the "corruptive" nature of the business world or a foray into new work that will express her character more fully. As such, Seeking is a strategy useful to attain life success, which may include career success. Seekers realize that their ability to find and express themselves will contribute to their personal satisfaction *and* the success of any venture in which they are involved. Women who are looking for a different job or a new career are not necessarily Seekers, however. Emulators might change jobs to improve their position on the corporate ladder, and Balancers might shift jobs to cut their work load so they can give more time to their home life. These kinds of job changes are merely tactical moves within a single success strategy.

Some women are lifelong Seekers. Others become temporary Seekers in order to move from one strategy to another; for example, from Emulator to Balancer or from Balancer to Integrator. Some move into the Seeker role just long enough to define their next step. It is also possible to be a Seeker concerned with self-definition while using one of the other success strategies to find career success.

The Story of a Seeker

Ann was not particularly popular in high school or college. Although she had a few friends, she was primarily a loner, a characteristic that worried her mother. Ann's father, however, would reassure them both that Ann was better off being herself than trying to get in with the popular crowd if that wasn't her inclination. Ann did not stand out in any way physically. Her height, build, brown hair, and eyes were all "medium." It was only after spending time getting to know her that I started to see her charm, liveliness, and concern for others. She had an inner light that was revealed only when she had come to know and trust me.

As a young woman, Ann loved to read and spent many hours engrossed in books about people, especially novels and biographies. In high school she began to think that her interest in how people lived might mean that she was destined for a career as a psychologist or social worker, although she had no definite idea of the kind of work those jobs might entail. In college Ann also became interested in Asian philosophies. On graduation she decided to pursue a career in recruiting.

She began her career as a recruiter's assistant in the personnel department of a major computer manufacturer. At the outset, she was focused on doing the best job she could. She worked many hours overtime and read everything she could get her hands on. As jobs opened up, she slowly began to move up in level and responsibility. During this time, Ann was content with her life. Although she had expected to marry early, that was the only part of her life that was not moving as she had anticipated. In general, she felt that she was learning and growing and was relatively pleased with her progress.

After several years with her company, Ann applied for the job of personnel manager in a small division in Houston, but the position went to a male colleague who was less experienced and less educated than she. She was told that the position required a person who was decisive and analytic. Since she had demonstrated both of these capabilities, she realized that the real issue was that she was not seen as "a comer." As a result of this setback, Ann decided to change her approach in order to bring her knowledge and commitment to management's attention. She studied how the most decisive and analytic men approached their careers and began to adopt those traits. She worked at being in control and taking a more bottom-line look at the business.

At first, the changes worked for Ann, and she quickly moved up the management chain. She began earning respect for her business ideas as well as for her understanding of the requirements of managing human resources. As time went on, however, she began to get the feeling (no one gave her any feedback) that she overwhelmed and even intimidated her colleagues and staff. Finally she was involved in a seemingly minor incident that became a critical turning point in her life. Ann had to fire a subordinate who had performed badly for a period of time.

After she gave what she thought was straight, direct feedback, the woman stared at her and shook her head sadly. "How can you be such a cold person?" the employee asked. Ann knew that the comment was partly a reaction to the bad news, but it seemed to contain a kernel of truth that bothered her. It was this incident that thrust Ann into the Seeker role.

In thinking about the criticism, Ann realized that she had developed a harsh, almost bitter persona in her quest for success. She wondered how she could have a cold personality at work and a warm one inside herself. She knew the real person was not the one she portrayed at work and decided to attend some company-sponsored workshops that she thought might help her find her true self.

The first workshop, "Improving Interpersonal Relationships," started her on a journey that lasted for the next eight years. She found that "new" information about herself often wasn't really news to her, but something she had been ignoring. For example, she found out that she was really a very nice person but had decided that "nice" wasn't going to get her anywhere at work, so she had covered up that part of her personality. She realized that she had made the incorrect assumption that being nice was inconsistent with being strong and decisive. The insight motivated her to explore some other beliefs and assumptions that had guided her actions.

From each workshop, conference, support group, counselor, and body worker, she learned something more about herself. She investigated the Myers-Briggs typology, neurolinguistic programming, the American Indian medicine wheel, yoga, and therapeutic massage. Slowly, she began to let herself and others know about the hidden parts of herself, such as the niceness. She began to discover a way to make the hard decisions she had to make and say things in an empathetic way. She began to feel more in tune with herself and found a calmness that she really liked.

When I spoke to her, Ann owned and ran her own computer reseller company in Dallas. In the course of her years of Seeking, Ann had realized she wanted to run her own business her own way. She continues to learn ways to be effective and authentic. She is careful to leave time for her family and friends and recently took a three-week backpacking trip through the Sierras, completely out of touch with her business. She and her company both gained from the experience.

Reflections on the Story of Ann

Ann demonstrated some of the qualities of a Seeker during her school years, with her interest in ideas, people, and philosophy. As she read, she applied these new concepts to her views on life. Her father was a substantial influence because he encouraged her to continue to explore and refine her natural style.

In her professional life Ann started out as a Trooper, but the experience of losing a desired job, one she felt strongly that she ought to have been given, propelled her into being an Emulator. In this transition,

Ann tried to develop a style that would make use of her strength and help her advance in her company. This is an example of someone attempting to exchange one strategy for another that will work more effectively. In the process, however, she unknowingly moved even further away from her own natural style and sense of herself.

Discovering that her new strategy was, in actuality, an uncomfortable choice turned out to be a useful lesson. When the subordinate she fired criticized her, Ann was able to see clearly that she had lost herself and was prepared to initiate a process to seek what she had lost.

For the next eight years, Ann primarily used the Seeker strategy, with her focus on her own internal growth, while at the same time she learned the business lessons she needed to progress. All the earlier groundwork, and even the reversal of direction, helped her to better understand herself. As she applied her lessons to her working life, Ann discovered not only the feminine compassion and niceness that were naturally hers, but also her true strength and ability to hold her own as an entrepreneur.

The Seeker's Worldview

As young women, Seekers often feel like underachievers. Two young M.B.A.s I interviewed feel they are destined for great success, but when they compare themselves with their classmates (invariably men), they are concerned that they have not yet started a business, made lots of money, or published their first book.

Seekers may feel a sense of frustration about themselves. One worked for a period in Japan, where she learned that the Japanese consider human relationships to be essential to achieving a goal, in contrast to the Western tendency to focus on the goal to the exclusion of relationships. She loved the independence and control she gained by being miles away from her boss and having to figure out what to do by herself. Yet she said,

> I feel like an underachiever. There is nothing I've done that I'm fully proud of. I get all kinds of positive feedback, but I have an

internal standard that tells me I'm not even in the ballpark yet. I'm finding it's more important to be who I am. I lived behind a mask for the past seven or eight years, and now I don't care what I give up to be myself.

The late thirties are a time of strategy transition for many women. That is when they realize that something has been missing from their lives, even after they have achieved some traditional success in their careers. At this point, many become Seekers and change their focus from traditional success to personal fulfillment. Some start businesses of their own, sometimes with a supportive husband or with other Seekers. Their explicit business goals reflect their Seeker nature; some will work only with clients who share their values or who expressly seek them out.

One Seeker, who had worked in the Emulator mode for many years, realized at the age of thirty-eight that she had "lopped off a portion" of herself:

I thought I was doing the right thing, but I started to realize I'd always felt something was wrong. I started to ask myself, what am I doing, what am I supporting, what am I building? Now I think, what kind of society am I helping to build?

Another woman who has been extremely successful in traditional terms, achieving partnership in a major consulting firm, has left the job to start her own company. At forty-two she is bothered by the fact that she feels out of synch with herself. "I don't seem to be very good at discovering my life's purpose," she says. The recent death of her brother has caused her to reflect more deeply on how she wants to live her life. She has become a Seeker, but one who as yet has no vocabulary or methodology for her search.

Seekers often take time off to consciously listen to themselves. A Seeker with a career in high-tech sales is looking for ways to express herself in her work:

Ultimately, I'd like to leave the business world and work with children in a creative way. Right now, I'm a single-person branch office, taking a sort of sabbatical from people, but I think I'll move to a small company next.

Women who are primarily Seekers choose their careers for the personal growth potential they offer. At the same time, they look to maximize their income and find situations that will utilize their intelligence, creativity, and experience. They see change as an opportunity for learning and are conscientious about keeping track of the patterns in their lives. All Seekers want "more," even if they don't know what "more" for them is. Usually it means more of themselves, regardless of how successful they have been in a material sense. A vice president in health care management said,

For a long time I felt split into multiple pieces—wife, mother, manager, bright, analytical, strong, gentle. I found I was sometimes inappropriate. I might be too soft at work or too tough at home. It's really over the last five years that I've been able to put it all together better. I see my life mission as integration—of myself and of our society. I want to bring peace to the planet. I view the jobs I do in terms of how they help me fulfill my mission. I still wrestle with a lack of confidence. I'm working on that. Also, I notice that when I have an overcontrolling manager, I have a rebellious inner child that gets me into trouble. I have to work on this. I do better with a large job and plenty of freedom.

A woman who recently started her own advertising agency revealed,

The path I'm on now is enabling myself to show more of myself. I'm more humble than I was. Now I feel more whole. I won't go back and do things the old way. I've been told I am serious, intense, and honest. I think I am not truly myself or really honest, but I think I am more than most. I couldn't have done this twenty years ago."

Self-Alignment for the Seeker

The Seeker, as a result of the seeking itself, has a greater measure of overlap between her conscious mind, her subconscious, and her higher self. The boundaries between these, however, are permeable, indicating that flux is possible in each element. Moreover, the Seeker is open to inputs in all three elements. In the process of seeking this access her higher self will expand, the direction for her life will become clear, and her outer circumstances will begin to show evidence of inner congruence.

The Seeker is often primarily focused on this journey, and while other work and family issues are important, the driving motivation is this search. Her choice is clear: to learn who she is and to be able to express that person in the world. Her self-talk may include such statements as:

- I am moving in the right direction.
- I am frustrated when I forget who I really am and play a role.
- I have no idea what I am doing, but it feels right and I can't stop.

The Seeker finds she gravitates toward other Seekers, including them in her circle of close friends. She may find a sense of sanity and safety in the company of others who share the special strife and rewards of her journey. She may begin to discover that people like her for who she is and that her colleagues sense a difference in her without being able to articulate what it is.

Advantages of the Seeker Approach

Seekers are generally successful in achieving their goals of self-discovery. They may find more than they had anticipated, but they will almost always discover something of personal value. A person who embarks on the road to self-discovery cannot control the results, but that is part of the beauty of the process. Whenever we think we have it all under control, we are bound to learn something to contradict that notion.

I went to a personal growth workshop by accident many years ago. This was the beginning of my search to feel more sane about my life. As such, it had a profound influence on the course of my life. (I've heard this from others as well. The first experience is often the most moving, since it opens up new territory.)

The title of this course was "Management Skills," and I was expecting to learn about such things as planning and delegating. Instead, the workshop was full of exercises that explored how we deal with conflict: how much of ourselves we disclose or hide, what our major motivation is in interactions, and what our personality types are. I had had no idea that such information had anything to do with managing.

As the week went on, I realized that finding out how to handle management situations was only a small portion of what there was for me to learn, and I felt excited and challenged. I very much liked those feelings and realized that I had not felt so vital in many years. This sense of vitality became the goal I held out for myself.

One night, I awoke at three in the morning full of excitement and ideas. In order not to disturb my roommate, I gathered up a blanket, a pillow, and my journal, and went into the bathroom. There I settled into the tub and wrote about my insights for hours. (Later, I found out that my roommate was also awake and wondering what on earth I was doing in the bath for so long.)

That one workshop opened up a new world for me. It led me to other modes of learning, a process that continues today. Finally, I began to see what I was doing that caused my feelings of dissatisfaction, my brusqueness, and my extreme need for control. I realized that I needed to associate myself with others who were conscious about how they lived their lives. I attended a number of similar workshops and finally went into therapy, thinking I was looking for a way to save my marriage, which was troubled. I discovered some harsh truths about myself, including the fact that I could no longer live with my husband and be true to myself.

I ended my marriage and then spent a year in extreme anguish, knowing I had done the right thing but feeling I had failed my

---

SEEKER CHECKLIST

Advantages	Disadvantages
Will achieve self-knowledge	Lessons may be hard ones
Results are satisfying	May find it hard to apply
Can apply lessons to work life	new information
Can influence the business	The process takes time
culture	May put career on the
	back burner

---

daughters, who were understandably upset by this change in their lives. And, of course, I felt I had failed in life. It was extremely painful to feel that the course I had taken was correct, yet not to be able to explain why. I had always relied on my logical mind, and when I made such a major shift in life circumstances based on intuition, I felt I ought to be able to tell others in clear, precise ways what I was doing and why. And I couldn't.

Today I have improved skills at using intuition, and I feel good about myself for doing so. I am more comfortable with ambiguity, yet I still battle my need for logical explanation (as if it would make everything OK). I have become more aware and more comfortable with my own process.

The Seeker feels good about herself when she is engaged in the process of her own search. Defusing her defenses and fears lifts a weight she may not even have realized she was carrying.

Disadvantages of the Seeker Approach

Seekers often find themselves developing an ability to intuit unspoken truths in many situations. Some may feel a sense of confusion about what they believe to be true and how to use this knowledge.

Sandra was encouraged by the culture in her company to ignore various problems that she saw with clarity. She mentioned several times that one employee was not good at her job and influenced others to do shoddy work. Since this older woman had a powerful position and had convinced others that she was necessary to the business, it was an unspoken rule that one did not criticize her. When the younger woman spoke the truth she saw, it was made clear to her that she had transgressed. She soon developed eye problems. In telling me about this situation, she said she believed her eye problems had occurred precisely because she was asked not to see what she actually saw.

Being castigated for truth telling can, indeed, have disastrous consequences. Women, especially, are prone to concentrate on the negative about themselves and ignore the positive. When we discover that we are liked or respected or admired, we need to be careful to absorb this positive feedback. Nonetheless, not all the useful information gathered by a Seeker will be positive. Here is what one interviewee had to say:

My first awareness of the need to journey inward happened ten years ago. I took a course in influence skills and got some feedback that I was very controlling. I was shocked! They didn't know who I was. How horrible the person they perceived was. I'd never heard of sharing power. I had no experience of it. I immediately started seeking other input. Since then, I've done a lot of personal growth work, looking to see what I wanted to do.

It can be difficult when we discover that others think us boring or inconsequential or unfeeling. It can be discouraging to discover some unlikable facet of our personality. But even this painful information can lead to important discoveries about ourselves. The message behind the criticism might indicate that our self-image is low or that we hold back from speaking the truth for fear of reprisal.

The insights that the Seeker gains may feel threatening at first. She may refuse to acknowledge some information, but will return to it and probe further as soon as she feels safe enough to do so. I have worked with people who one day would glimpse things about themselves that opened wonderful new possibilities they had never before imagined. The next day, I would find them closed down again, as if they could absorb only so much at one time.

> When I attended that first personal growth seminar, I was at first dismayed with all the work that it seemed I would have to do. And I did not have a clue as to how to attempt some of the changes I felt I needed to make. Soon, however, I realized that I was applying my old patterns to my new perceptions. I had always felt that once I became aware of a problem, I should immediately address it with great energy. Problems were to be solved, and the sooner the better. With my newfound awareness, I began to realize that what I perceived as a series of problems was nothing of the kind. In fact, my life was not a total disaster, as I had for a short time believed; I was fine inside, although there were aspects that I felt a need to modify. I began to realize that I had uncovered a series of areas that would improve with further growth, none of which needed to be attacked immediately. Of course, I did attack some of them right away, but you can't change everything at once.

Seeking *is* a lifelong endeavor; it does *not* all need to be done at once. It is not even possible to integrate everything we learn about ourselves immediately; it takes time. We have to disassemble our defenses slowly so that we do not feel overly vulnerable.

A Seeker may find that she is temporarily disconnected from her former anchors. In moving toward a new aspect of her personality, she has to weaken or eliminate contradictory patterns. An Emulator, for example, who believes that she is decisive and hard may have to allow the possibility that she is also soft and ambivalent at times to enter her mind slowly. As she perceives previously unacknowledged characteristics, she may feel as if she has no self-definition she can count on, and losing a sense of the familiar can be quite disconcerting. Learning something that challenges the concept we have of ourselves nearly always requires that we at least consider throwing out some aspect of that former structure. Learning is change, and change is required for life.

Seekers often slow their pace of achievement in the business world while they are in the process of learning about themselves. Some Seekers develop such enthusiasm for their journey that they pay little attention to other aspects of their lives. Several women who are or had been Seekers told me that they allowed their careers to take second place while they were in a brief but intense search. For most, however, the journey becomes simply one aspect of their lives, to be integrated with all the others.

The Value of Congruity

Merely by engaging in the Seeking process, a woman is discovering greater self-alignment. We must know or sense who we are in order to operate in tune with our true nature. That knowledge is not something we learn in our heads; we must feel it in our hearts. It is an inner knowing, not an external fact we can memorize. Facts change, or we forget them, or they are superseded by other facts. Knowing, or *gnosis*, provides a constant path toward our selves.

Our sense of who we are will continue to grow as we become aware of different aspects of ourselves and are able to put pieces together across the years. Perhaps you had terrible arguments with your parents when you were young because they had rules for your behavior that you resisted. Later, when you become a supervisor, you might find yourself imposing structure on your subordinates that is really not needed. You may discover you absorbed from your parents the notion that there are rules for everything and that rules provide safety. Or you may learn that you resist structure when it is imposed on you, but that you rather like imposing it on others. You may learn something about anger or love or independence. These kinds of discoveries will be different for each individual, but the Seeker will continue to learn greater and greater truth about herself.

What is the value of this search? Knowing who you are leads to more congruent behavior. Thus, when we feel anger, it does not become rage; it is limited to the specific situation, we are able to express it appropriately, and then we move on without residue. When we understand that we believe rules provide safety, we are able to consciously explore which rules do this and which are in place simply because we once accepted the notion that all rules are good or that authorities are supposed to provide rules. Then as employees, we react in concert with rules that make sense, we question those that do not, and we go along with those that someone made up to serve their own ego but that have no negative impact on us. In other words, when we know ourselves well, our behavior is consistent with our deeper purpose in life and we do not become entangled with issues that have nothing to do with us. Why waste energy?

Congruent behavior communicates a powerful message without words. Science has established that when words and actions are disparate, we believe the actions. "Do as I say and not as I do" has long been recognized as a ridiculous statement. Ultimately, what you do is far more powerful than what you say. Would you prefer to follow a leader who deeply believes in her message, or one who merely says the right words and smiles nicely?

Leader or follower, we are more effective when our words and actions are congruent. But there is a deeper level of congruence that is even more important and has greater impact on others. That is when our words and actions are congruent with knowing and expressing who we really are. I have written of many of the women I interviewed who express this congruence in their lives.

The woman who is a director of her company and in line to be CEO is not motivated by power or status. She truly believes in her company, wants to provide a service to her clients, and knows she will lead in an inspired way. The woman who left the corporate world to become a personal growth counselor is successful in her work because she is committed to responding to her clients from the deepest part of herself. She tells the truth in a way that enriches and challenges them. The woman who toured China for a year is an inspired graphic designer who draws clients from across the country without advertising. Not only do people want to work with her, but she is able to perceive the intent of what they want to express and develop designs that convey that message strongly.

A Seeker strives for congruent behavior, which is the outward manifestation of self-alignment. It is communicated without words. Individuals who are congruent are able to deal with the many stresses of business life without becoming depleted. They are already demonstrating a great measure of integration.

8

The Integrator

The Integrator is a woman who has at her disposal all her skills, attributes, wisdom, and insights. She is clear about who she is and values expressing herself with congruity of word, action, and being. This clarity is extremely powerful. Those who know and work with Integrators often remark on the exceptional consistency of their values and actions. The Integrator truly enjoys being female and finds feminine ways to demonstrate her assertiveness, power, and competency. Her managers, peers, and subordinates all trust and value her combination of ability and authority. She is very successful in both traditional terms (salary, level, power) and in terms of the entire fabric of her life. An Integrator is a woman who enjoys, and is successful at, expressing herself as a whole person.

Integrators are aware of the requirements of the traditional business system and are able to adapt to it without compromising themselves as women. For example, they are able to be assertive or confrontive when necessary, while at the same time showing their empathy. They know how to collaborate and still ensure that the power structure is aware of their accomplishments. While maintaining a balanced management presence, they are invariably able to bring their own unique style to bear

129

on any situation. One Integrator, president of a construction company, is known for being a hugger. On greeting or taking leave of business colleagues, she will give each a quick hug. She says that people were taken aback at first, but that she is sure that now they rather look forward to this bit of personal acknowledgment and contact.

Integration is a strategy because for many it is a conscious choice arising from a desire to be successful and be whole. Choosing to use all of yourself at work is, for some, a difficult decision. The culture of the workplace does not necessarily encourage wholeness.

Superficially, the Integrator is similar to the Balancer. Both use an effective combination of feminine and masculine skills and behaviors in their business dealings. The difference lies in the openness of the communication channels within. The Balancer has *learned* to combine two different roles; that combining is an acquired skill. The Integrator combines roles naturally, as an expression of who she really is. Hers is a true integration—a subtle and qualitative harmony—not an acquired set of behaviors. Most of us are able to intuit which women are Integrators and which Balancers. The subtle differences are apparent. Balancers may be competent and successful, but we instinctively recognize Integrators; they command our respect. Here are quotes from two very successful Integrators:

> I have very good communication skills and use humor well. I have a high degree of personal charm and know how to use it. I hate manipulation—I don't do this. I have a lot of energy around leadership and achievement. I also love the female stuff. I had lots of women in my early life as well as a strong father. Mostly, I get to do what I think is best. I may lose a battle, but I know how to pull back and come back again. People should not have to guess who you are—they should *see* it. I believe in doing what you say you are going to do. I believe I work for my people, not that they work for me.

> I'm treated reasonably well. I don't have to be a dual personality—I can be who I am. I know I'm successful; my definition

comes from within. It's hard to set our own standards because we are often hardest on ourselves. My husband is a big cheerleader, plus I have several true friends. People feel confident in me; they feel they can depend on me. At one point my colleagues did not value what I do (fundraising). I spoke to them about the importance of giving. After that they appreciated my contribution to the university and to the community. What's important to me is what I believe in.

I have presented the five success strategies to a number of groups and generally conclude my speech with a question-and-answer segment. During one such period, the conversation moved to the Integrator. There are often questions regarding the difference between the Integrator and the Balancer. For someone who has never considered self-alignment or is only beginning their quest, the two strategies may seem the same. For those who have traveled the path of self-knowledge and self-esteem, the difference is more apparent.

One man in the audience raised his hand, and when I called on him, he said simply, "I once worked for a woman who was an Integrator." His tone of voice suggested that he had been deeply touched by this woman. She seemed to have enabled him to see parts of himself he had never before considered. He added that she had encouraged all her subordinates to challenge themselves and had provided a "leadership energy" as he called it, that made the department an exciting place to work. The attitude of the audience shifted as they suddenly understood the concept of the Integrator. It was as though people thought, "Oh, you mean *that* kind of woman." The questioning moved on and, sadly, I never learned more. I wanted to know about her and the impact she had on others.

There are two types of Integrators. Early Integrators know themselves from a young age and are able to express their self-alignment with growing ability as their careers advance. Katherine Hepburn is a good example of an Early Integrator. While these people have to learn the skills of their chosen profession, they are secure in who they are.

Late Integrators struggle into integration as they progress in their careers; they have to work consciously at achieving and maintaining their self-alignment. Tina Turner, as portrayed in the movie *What's Love Got to Do With It*, exemplifies a Late Integrator. Many of us have come to integration later in life and have to work at keeping at bay the devils that tell us we are being self-centered or prideful when we achieve a solid sense of ourselves and operate from that center.

In the following two stories, Maria is an Early Integrator and Ann a Late Integrator. We met Ann, the Seeker, in Chapter Seven. She became an Integrator after moving through several of the other success strategies.

The Story of Maria

Maria is a tall, slim woman with long, dark, shiny hair. She grew up in a large family. Although they were not well off, her parents managed to give their children the material things they really needed. More important, they focused on developing each child's unique personality and gave each one a sense of being loved. One brother, who weathered much early teasing from his schoolmates because of his interest in the arts, became a professional musician with his parents' support. A sister competed at the national level on a women's volleyball team. The whole family attended her games together.

Maria wanted to attend a women's college and was able to find enough scholarship money to make that possible. There, her already developed self-esteem and sense of self-importance were supported and encouraged. She was elected president of several student groups, which helped her realize that she had an easy leadership style. She was egalitarian with her group members and had a good command of their overall goals. She was able to inspire her followers to willingly exert themselves to accomplish group goals. People seemed to flock around her and offered to work on her committees. She said she was proud of the fact that this continued throughout her career.

Maria acknowledged to herself that she was smart, ambitious, and competitive, and decided to study for an M.B.A. and go into business. After graduate school, she quickly found a position in an information systems group responsible for providing technical support to a financial team. Maria often wrote programs for clients who had no desire to learn such skills, but she preferred to work with those who wanted to learn to program for themselves. She believed that programming would give employees a better grasp of their business. At that time she had no words for what she instinctively believed to be the most effective as well as most efficient approach. She discovered later that her approach was a form of self-empowerment.

Maria's empowerment approach brought her into conflict with her management. Management was concerned that if everyone created their own sets of numbers, no one would know which numbers were right and the company would have no way to control its business. Maria countered that it certainly would not be difficult to create and implement standards that would allow employees freedom of computing while protecting data integrity.

In response to her opinionated "meddling," Maria was offered a position in a newly formed group responsible for creating computing and documentation standards. She soon realized that the job was offered because her outspokenness had annoyed management and they wanted her in a position where they could control her. They thought she had potential but would be more valuable if she came around to their way of thinking.

In her new group, Maria quickly became a prominent advocate for developing standards in partnership with those who would use them, and she was encouraged to find that other group members felt as she did. As her boss had hoped, Maria did begin to learn about the complexity involved in making substantial changes in an organization.

In time, Maria was able to temper her enthusiasm with her new knowledge. She became a convincing spokesperson for the group's innovative approach. She was able to meet challenges, learn from her mistakes, and change her approach as needed. She felt that she had to proceed on her own terms to do what was right and natural for her, but at the same time she realized that she had much to learn. She loved the process of growing ever more sophisticated in her ability to express what was important to her.

Today, Maria is a vice president and chief information officer for her company, responsible for all computing decisions. Under her oversight, the company has made extensive use of personal computers, using a set of standards that are reviewed yearly by a group of managers from each major department. As a result, the company has saved countless dollars in expense and Maria's peers credit her with creating several innovative solutions that have increased market share and revenue.

Maria continues to use her own outspoken yet persuasive style to challenge old concepts and to sell new ideas. She is considered a creative, high-energy, enthusiastic woman who also exhibits a strong preference for joint decision making and a collaborative style. She is an extremely valued member of the senior management team, and other corporations often try to recruit her.

The Story of Ann

As a child, encouraged by her father, Ann learned to follow her own inclinations instead of merely going along with the crowd. Early on, she appreciated the importance of getting to know herself through active exploration and by trying out behaviors to see which ones felt right to her. In those years she developed an ability for critical thinking that continued throughout her life.

After years in business, frustrated with "thrashing around," Ann moved into the Seeker strategy, pursuing self-exploration as much as possible in order to find a business style that would be both successful and reflective of her true nature. While that was her original motivation, she soon found she was learning about far deeper aspects of herself than she had expected to find.

As a natural result of seeking, she moved into being an Integrator. She had learned, for example, that she liked to please others and to have all the right answers before she was even asked. Ann also became aware of her tendency to take criticism personally and to worry about whether others would like her if she didn't do what they wanted and expected.

As she moved further into the Integrator category, she discovered that these aspects of her personality could be applied to great advantage in dealing with customers and employees. She consciously planned ahead for meetings with others, anticipating the issues and questions that might arise. She learned not to allow her desire to please others to control her actions.

Recently Ann was engaged in negotiating a joint venture with a man who had developed a software package she felt would be extremely useful to her clients. During the negotiation process, Ann found that she was on the verge of giving her partner a greater share of the potential profits than he deserved because he was so forceful in expressing the value of his product. She realized that he needed her to open up the market as much as she needed him to provide the product. When she suggested a more equitable proposal, he reacted with anger and threatened to take his product elsewhere. Ann was able to hold firm in the face of his reaction and show him that dealing with her would benefit them both and that she was not about to give away the store. He quickly saw her point and, although he was not pleased, he was impressed with her business savvy and willingly signed the agreement.

Ann was careful about hiring new employees and usually knew in the first interview or two whether an applicant would fit into her organization. If she made a mistake, she invariably discovered it within the probation period. She trusted her intuition and had not had to fire anyone in many years. She was able to offer her employees critical feedback and did it in a way that enabled them to gain from the experience. They invariably walked out of her office agreeing with her and feeling challenged to improve their performance. They were moved, challenged, and excited by her. Ann told me that many times her employees had thanked her for her helpful criticism and told her that they had imitated her style to good advantage.

Over the years, Ann has done more than learn how to complement her natural skills with acquired ones. Today, as an Integrator, she knows how to render her feminine power, strength, and unique characteristics more available to herself and to others. She understands herself well enough that she can catch herself in unnecessary defensive or destructive behavior patterns and reverse them quickly. She doesn't dwell on her mistakes because that only wastes energy. She has developed a powerful way of operating in the business world that is based on the truth of who she really is.

Ann perceives her career as a wonderful game. She said she wakes up in the morning feeling excited about the prospects of the coming day. She is successful in the business world and feels that her whole life is extremely satisfying and fulfilling. She continues to learn more about herself every day.

Her search to more completely comprehend her inner truth is the key to her authenticity. Looking for more than a mental understanding of her emotional traits and energy, she has sought to grasp her spiritual aspect as well. She spoke to me about the power of prayer and said that her connection to God has served to strengthen her own natural skills. She feels as though she is doing what God wants her to do and that through her job she has the opportunity to help make the world a better place.

Reflections on the Stories of Maria and Ann

Both Maria and Ann demonstrate qualities of the Integrator. They know their own minds, feel confident in their opinions, are respected and valued in their companies, and have an easy feminine style supported by an inner strength. They are able to relate to people at all levels in their organizations. They appear comfortable, centered, and unflappable. As Integrators, Maria and Ann are able to make hard business decisions with grace, humor, and determination. They are appealing without being sexual. People like to be around them and vie to work for them.

Even with their extensive inner resources, Integrators do not have perfect lives. They experience their share of difficulty and often fall into old patterns of behavior or thinking that are defensive, limiting, or even destructive. Integrators, like all people, have to fight their own dragons. Over time the Integrator's battles begin to have less and less impact on them. And they see the battles coming and gain control earlier. Thus, instead of feeling as though they are valueless or incompetent for months, Integrators may be able to rid themselves of these feelings in a short time—perhaps hours or even minutes.

One Late Integrator confessed, "I stay open to enormous amounts of data, except in crisis. Then I focus down to get the information I need to survive." That she knows this about herself makes it possible for her to recognize when she is in a crisis mode and to remind herself that her process is really OK. Another senior vice president of a major distribution company said that recovery from a mistake had impressed her to learn more about herself and improve her skills.

> I had this major learning years ago. I was new on the management committee and at the first strategic planning session, the guy in charge of planning made a terrible presentation. It was sloppy, and clearly he wasn't prepared well. The department head stopped him. And here's what impressed me: he completely changed his approach, asked the group what they wanted, and got them to brainstorm some planning ideas. I've never seen a better bounce-back. I realized I could never have done that, but I learned that vulnerability combined with confidence is tremendously valuable. Now when there is a mistake, I'm calm and say I'll fix it.

Integrators report that being true to themselves is both a successful strategy and personally fulfilling. Yet finding one's stride is a process of discovery. An Integrator who was formerly an Emulator described how early in her career she had difficulty in modifying herself to fit in. "I got along in spite of being myself. I didn't constrain myself to behave in a narrow bandwidth." She went on to say that it was some time before she realized that the traditional business route wasn't right for her. She is now very successfully running her own consulting and training business and finds a balance with her personal life by deliberately booking time to be home with her daughter.

Another Integrator, who is extremely competent and could certainly do a much bigger job, decided that she wanted to schedule more time for her personal interests, so she deliberately got off the fast track.

> I'm good, but I'm not threatening, so the other executives trust me. I can relate more comfortably if they know I'm a whole person. I was voted onto the management committee. I think it's because I absolutely know the business and because I don't play games (male ones or female ones). I have been very successful, but recently I decided to back off. I have been recruited many times for a great deal of money, but I got off the leading-edge track—the price was too high. I go home at six or seven in the evening and I have cut back on public speaking. Now my job is totally manageable. I'm very satisfied. I never dreamt I could achieve as much as I have.

A key manager of a large service firm says that she is absolutely committed to being true to herself. Her goal is to create an environment in which every employee has the capacity to be as happy and as successful as they can be.

> I try to tell the truth as I see it. People should be able to see who you are. But I do it tactfully, with consideration of feelings. Also, I do what I say I'm going to. This develops trust. Business is business, but no business operates without people.

The Early Integrator

The Early Integrator has always had a clear sense of who she is and has probably come from a supportive family environment. She may have been educated at a women's college. When speaking with Early Integrators, one is instantly aware of the easy clarity and self-alignment they exhibit. They do not generally refer to it themselves because it is so natural to them.

Early Integrators bring all their feminine skills to their jobs. In addition, they train themselves to think strategically, make quick decisions, and take command when necessary; this helps them achieve excellence in their fields. Thus, although they have not had to overcome early dis-integration, Early Integrators work hard to learn the skills required in their chosen career.

They may find that colleagues who have not worked with them before do not believe they are as straightforward as they truly are. The Early Integrator may be distrusted simply because others expect that the solid, secure sense of self she portrays is an act.

Unlike Late Integrators, Early Integrators do not generally pay much attention to male/female working issues. They are not blind to them, nor do they think that other women are making up or exaggerating their experiences. They just don't find sexism a compelling issue. Early Integrators regard themselves as lucky in this regard. They are able to be themselves in any situation.

> One young woman told me that she has found that many in the business world behave as though there is a hierarchy in every relationship, and she tolerates being in the "one down" position at first in a new business relationship. Generally, she said, most managers prefer to be the one who is "up." Rather than fight this, she simply remains steady and secure in her knowledge that she is an equal without saying or doing anything differently. I do not agree that she is letting herself be "one down." I think what she does differently is refuse to try to be "one up." As people talk to her, they talk themselves into their own vulnerability. Then she can help them. She does not force the issue, she just is herself and lets that essence work. There is no need to do more.

Early Integrators make outstanding managers and business leaders (when they choose to). One Integrator, in line to be CEO of an East Coast consulting firm, described her strategy as being absolutely committed to a few carefully chosen values: managing people and the systems that support them, telling the truth tactfully, focusing on the big picture, and always doing what she says.

It seems that it takes a woman thirty years or so to settle into the role of Integrator. All the Integrators in this study ranged in age from thirty-seven to seventy. Early Integrators all report that they had been themselves, not playing a role, for as long as they could remember, but it is difficult to recognize the attributes of an Integrator early in her career. All the Integrators I interviewed were extremely successful in traditional terms and considered themselves satisfied and happy.

The Late Integrator

The Late Integrator has arrived at self-alignment after exploring other success strategies. She has had to work to achieve a measure of integration. After perfecting the skills of the Balancer, for example, she may find she still has an internal desire for more. Most Late Integrators have found their way by employing various personal growth modalities.

Late Integrators often speak in terms of the difference between masculine and feminine energy, rather than about the differences between men and women. They are aware that men as well as women are controlled by a system that arbitrarily relegates all assertiveness, competitiveness, and business acumen to men and all nurturing and responsibility for relationships to women. While they understand the system, they often feel a responsibility to contribute to changing it. One Late Integrator said:

> I did a lot of modifying of myself while trying to stay authentic. I did a two-year overseas assignment. It was helpful because I looked fear in the face—the worst that could happen did. When I came back, here I was having this life-changing experience, but

no one seemed interested. Finally, I decided to tell a few important people. One man listened intently and told me I didn't look any different. Everything I had discovered about myself he already knew. The mind-blower was that I had learned and accepted it.

Now I live thinking, "How should I carry out my responsibility for being my true self and living in an honorable way?" I started to see a real limit to my ambition. Now I'm not driven by thoughts of the next title. I slowed down and I'm very interested in finding ways to work with young and college-age girls.

While Early Integrators take their self-alignment more in stride, Late Integrators tend to stay conscious of how they have had to adapt to survive and the impact that adaptation has had on their skills and emotions. Many have experienced difficult or even abusive childhoods. They continue to struggle with their self-esteem and with maintaining their integrity in a world that is not itself integrated. One Late Integrator told me that part of her envied the Early Integrators, but she was not sure that she would have given up the struggle she had endured because of the tremendous value it had afforded her in the long run.

Self-Alignment for the Integrator

Integrators are not perfectly aligned every moment of the day. They have acquired the skills to realign themselves when they slip out of focus. The self-talk of the Integrator may sound like this:

- I have an internal process that rescues me when I fall into old patterns.
- I am excited about my life and about the way I am living it.
- I really do have valuable skills to give to the world.
- I feel as though I am doing what I am supposed to do.

The Integrator may, upon occasion, question her own value or skills or intelligence, but she is generally able to use the questioning as a trigger to renew her alignment.

INTEGRATOR CHECKLIST

Advantages	Disadvantages
Has achieved self-knowledge	Has to keep working at
Has a positive influence on others	maintaining self-
Feels competent and confident	alignment
Influences the business culture	May feel uncomfortable
	with visibility or envy

The Integrator gets along very well with most people. She has close friends and family. There may be people in her life who are intimidated by her strength, particularly those who envy her. But the Integrator is generally able to confront people in a way that supports them; thus she can be an extremely powerful manager. Her external reality is a close representation of her inner voice and her purpose in life.

The Key Issues for Integrators

Staying self-aligned requires diligence, even for Early Integrators. Many have to remind themselves continually to look within for their answers and not to worry about advice, opinions, and counsel of others. Like most women, Integrators are influenced by what are considered to be appropriate roles for women. They may struggle to operate in a way that is consistent with their inner selves. One woman put it this way:

> We've built a society that has left off the feminine values with a single-minded focus on profitability. Lately, lots of men and women are exploring alternatives—creating different institutions. Now many women have gone into business. They are discovering they had left off a piece of themselves. The issue is how to integrate. I'm interested in personal exploration and also in business. As I approached forty, I started to merge these two ideas. I do a lot of pro bono work and I donate a portion of my profits to an organization for peace.

I value my own expertise and experience. I work at letting go of the old ways of operating in business and at overcoming myself. You set up mental models and try to operate that way. Then you come to boundaries and have to stretch. Sometimes I feel as though a boundary is reality and I can't get beyond it. It's hard to own up to it being an obstacle I manufactured in my mind. It takes real courage to be honest with yourself.

Integrators who march to the beat of their own drummer become more visible. Some feel uncomfortable with their uniqueness, yet at the same time they relish it. Using inner wisdom as a source of effectiveness is addictive in a positive way. The more we do it, the more motivated we are to continue the process. There is a built-in reward system for being self-aligned. It feels comfortable and easy. In fact, Integrators report that, over time, it becomes difficult to pretend to be something other than who they are.

One evening recently I gave a talk about my work at a professional society meeting. I had reviewed my slides with a male colleague prior to the event, and had taken some of his advice and ignored some. I made the choices based on what I felt was natural to my presentation style. (I did not feel comfortable with a bulleted list of gender differences, for example. I did feel comfortable with pictures and stories to illustrate my points.)

During the evening, I told a number of tales about myself and the women I had interviewed. I joked about some of the ways in which we all trap ourselves. I could feel the audience was right with me, following my points and feeling the emotions of their own stories. Some time afterward a woman thanked me for my honesty about my struggles and successes. "A woman came to me for advice yesterday," she said. "I know I was more helpful because I had your speech in mind. You have influenced my outlook a great deal."

It has taken me years to feel comfortable being myself, saying what I know, laughing about my mistakes, and finding my way to contribute to others. I now find it difficult to operate in any other way.

Self-alignment increases both competence and self-confidence. As Late Integrators move toward greater self-alignment, they find that their ability to trust themselves improves. Early Integrators typically have a greater measure of innate self-confidence than the rest of us, and their confidence deepens and becomes easily accessible as they mature. Thus, when learning a new skill, the Integrator may start with confidence and build competence, or first become adept at the task and let confidence grow with her ability (recall the competence-confidence model in Chapter Five). Furthermore, she is less likely to fall back over the line into low confidence. If she does, she returns more easily and quickly to a state of high confidence.

Integrators are comfortable with their femininity. They do not find themselves twisting into a pretzel to meet others' expectations.

One young Integrator, who has a compelling femininity, incurred a serious injury to the ligaments in her wrist as a result of a fall from a galloping horse while on a mountain-climbing trip in Africa. After her return, she attended a business meeting wearing a wrist brace. One of the "old guard" asked her how she had injured herself. His response, when she told him the story, was an astonished, "And I always thought you were so feminine." This young woman exemplifies a new version of "feminine"—a woman who is comfortable with her femininity but who isn't afraid to participate in activities regardless of how masculine they might seem.

All women (and men) have "integration" experiences. Most eight- to ten-year-old girls are unconscious Integrators. Emily Hancock, in *The Girl Within* (1989), describes how girls of this age frequently experience the strength and power of a well-aligned person only to fall prey to the strictures of society within the next several years. We then, says

Hancock, spend the rest of our lives trying to recover that "girl within." We all have within us a memory and experience of integration that, if accessed, allows us to rediscover ourselves. There are times for all of us when everything comes together easily and quietly and we are able to accomplish a difficult task that expresses who we are. For those who desire to increase their measure of integration, the process is one of discovering what already exists rather than learning something new. It is a "letting go" of the learned adaptations that no longer serve us, in order to reveal an already fully formed sense of self.

William Bridges' description of change in *Transitions* (1980) still stands as a useful and comforting model. He suggests that there are three stages in changing. The first is letting go of the old, the second is the "confusing nowhere of in-betweenness," and the last is settling into the new.

When we have let go of an old self-definition we must patiently proceed through the transition stage in which we release the old and begin to define the new, rather than try to rush immediately into a new definition. In that process we find a clearer sense of ourselves, not a completely different person. It is akin to the example of the woman who had a life-changing experience and, when she described what she had learned, was told that people already knew that about her.

In integrating, we move into knowing more deeply who we already are, even if that was a secret we kept from ourselves. Then we are challenged to express ourselves in the world in our own unique way. We may express ourselves quietly, in our being or creativity, or publicly, in entrepreneurship, the corporate structure, or even politics. Each woman must listen to herself to know what self-expression is right for her.

There is an old tradition of "coming out" parties for young women. These are large formal dances at which the debutantes are "presented" to society. Today, many women find the "coming out" concept superficial and a bit degrading, as if women are products to be placed on display when they are finished. Yet, if we contemplate the original intent, setting aside the limited historical role of women, there is a parallel to the process of becoming an Integrator. Presentation at a debutante party signaled to the world that a woman was ready to take her place as a complete, responsible adult. Becoming integrated is also a process of recognition; it is a way of acknowledging who we are and of making ourselves visible as whole, responsible, adult women.

Early Integrators find it easier than the rest of us to access their sense of self. Late Integrators are motivated to find ways to return to their buried sense of self. Seekers are preparing for their "coming out." For all of us, taking our place as whole, responsible, powerful, feminine beings is the most important work we can do for ourselves, for our companies, and for our society.

PART THREE

How to Increase Self-Alignment

9

Discovering Self-Alignment:
Awareness, Acceptance, Action

How do I achieve greater self-alignment and authenticity?" This is the question most people ask when they perceive a difference between where they are and where they would like to be. It is useful to be aware of different approaches as well as the limitations inherent in any such process.

When our conscious mind, subconscious, and higher self communicate, more resources and knowledge become available to us. For example, in gaining self-alignment, one woman might become aware that she prefers to be more introverted, which would help her realize that she might not find life satisfying as a high school teacher but might as a writer. Another might conclude that since she wants to work personally with individuals, she will go into training or counseling rather than stay on the corporate fast track. A third might see that her desire to make a difference in the world can best be fulfilled by developing a unique product and starting her own business, which she could run using her own style. Yet another might decide that big business needs her special approach and feel challenged by moving up the corporate ladder.

Increasing self-alignment by increasing access to all our skills, attributes, and wisdom can be perceived as a process that involves three elements: awareness, acceptance, and action. To be true to ourselves, we must be able to listen to ourselves, accept what we know to be true, and find ways to act on this intuition. In this way, we increase the resources we have available and strengthen our ability to ensure that they are all engaged toward a common goal. This is not always easy because sometimes we seem to be urged to embark on a course of action we perceive as beyond our control or our abilities.

Most of this chapter is devoted to a discussion that can lead to self-alignment and the three elements of self-alignment: awareness, acceptance, and action.

Paths and Traps

There are a wide variety of approaches that different people have found useful in the quest for self-alignment. I recommend that you choose one that fits your style. You may find a church group focused on the use of prayer an excellent way to feel the God inside yourself, or you may enroll in some of the multitude of personal growth programs available. Some find a path of service beckons them; they devote themselves to accomplishing whatever they can to help others whether that be in nursing, writing a book, or starting a company dedicated to expressing their own moral principles.

Numerous people have found personal and spiritual truth from being involved in a twelve-step program. Many Eastern religious and philosophical disciplines have been successfully adapted to Western use; a variety of forms of meditation such as transcendental meditation (TM), zazen (a Zen discipline of sitting), and tai chi (a structured set of movements) are among the best known. Some find body work such as Feldenkrais, Rolfing, or Reiki useful. Others respond to working with a teacher or guide.

Ram Dass points out that the use of any of these paths is an interesting exercise in itself. Any path, he says, will gain you what you seek if your desire is great enough. In order to make the best use of the path, you will need to fully involve yourself. Having done that, however, any path can become a trap because it is easy to think that the magic is in the path itself. In order to find and express our "selves," we must pour ourselves wholeheartedly into that path until we have gained enough substance to see that *we* are the magic, and the path is only a path.

As we learn to listen to the wisdom communicated from the higher self, it will tell us the next step to take and the next after that. Those steps will be different for everyone. Thus, neither I nor anyone can prescribe a precise approach for someone else. We must each find it for ourselves. I can, however, suggest some actions to take and some ideas to contemplate that may lead toward the beginning of an answer.

Increasing the degree of communication between the conscious mind, the subconscious, and the higher self, regardless of the path you choose, will require attention to the three steps of self-alignment. Depending upon your success strategy, you may have more difficulty with one than another.

Awareness

The first step in establishing a dialogue with the higher self is to quiet the conscious mind in order to become aware of the subconscious when it reports information, messages of support, or suggestions for action or contemplation. We already know far more than we realize, but we must give the subconscious a change to convey its messages from the higher self. We are then free to use this intuition to make decisions.

My husband and I were both immersed in our consulting careers when we lived on the East Coast. Then we decided to move to Colorado and I took on the task of coordinating the move, reducing considerably my consulting load. I planned to start working again once I had our house in order.

After settling in, however, I found that what I really wanted to do was to sit on top of my mountain and listen to myself. I worked on consulting projects part of the time, but they never seemed to be as interesting as my sitting. I literally spent time sitting—sometimes reading, sometimes meditating. Often I would wander down the hill to our meditation bench. This handmade two-person wooden bench is placed at the top of a rock cliff. There is a rock in front of the bench that I can use as a footstool. It is very comfortable. From there I have a clear view of the Continental Divide. There I would let the silence and the sense of vastness fill me up.

I am a hiker. Part of my process of listening includes climbing the local mountains. When I lived on the East Coast, I climbed all the mountains in New Hampshire that were higher than four thousand feet. As I climbed, I would keep in mind the summit—my goal. Colorado was different. When you start climbing at eight thousand feet, you can't think about much except your need for oxygen. I've discovered that I have to stay in the present moment in order to climb in the West. Each step is happening now. I have a goal in mind, of course, but the only reality I am aware of is the present: "Here is an almost level place, how nice; here the aspens have taken over; here it is dark and quiet; here it is steep and the path is washed out." Here and here and here. Hiking in the West has improved my ability to remain focused on the present moment. Only in this way can I know myself.

I was conscious of a need to remain in the present and to listen for the quiet voice inside. I kept waiting for pictures or words to come to me, preferably words, preferably clearly articulated ones. I hoped these words would tell me what I should do next.

At first, all I sensed was a feeling of deep peacefulness—no words, darn it. I wondered if that meant that I was retired, although that didn't seem right. I questioned myself: Had I failed at my career? Was that why I didn't seem to have much work? Of course, I did neither networking nor marketing, so that probably wasn't right. Had I just lost interest in working? Maybe—the feeling kept coming to me— maybe I am supposed to be doing a different sort of work.

I kept listening and soon became aware of a vast sense of energy. I knew then that I had to get to work; but what to do? I continued to tune into my inner urgings that sought expression, and I waited some more—a year altogether—to uncover the next step in my career—a step that was a direct outcome of the communication with my higher self.

Perhaps if I were better attuned to myself, I could have accomplished this transition in less than a year. But perhaps not. Timing is as individual as purpose.

We generally use our conscious mind to figure out our lives. In doing so, we are dealing with what the Buddhists call "the ordinary mind." The ordinary mind believes it must be in charge, so if we allow the higher self to take over, our ordinary mind is likely to give us exceptionally good reasons for returning to *its* control. Sogyal Rinpoche (1992, 46) says, "The ordinary mind is the ceaselessly shifting and shiftless prey of external influences, habitual tendencies, and conditioning."

The Buddhists teach there is another aspect of mind, termed the "essential nature of mind." Of this, Sogyal Rinpoche says, "Then there is the very nature of mind, its innermost essence, which is absolutely and always untouched by change or death" (p. 47). Other writers have referred to this inner knowledge as God, the Self, Shiva, or Higher Guidance. If we quiet the ordinary mind enough, we can become aware of ourselves as more than we normally think we are. We are then open to hearing our own truth at a very deep level. This truth will reveal our *dharma*, or the correct actions for us to take.

Nelson (1993) refers to the ordinary mind as the personality or ego. She writes of the search for awareness of her true self and the seeming conflicts between her true self and her personality. She states that her personality tried to keep her from acting according to her true self. "The magic was that everything higher guidance told me and showed me ultimately turned out to be true, even against seemingly impossible odds. And in spite of my personality's repeated warnings, I did not go broke, I did not die, and I did not end up crazy or alone" (p. 9).

Taking the advice of higher guidance feels as though we have let go of control of our lives. Since Westerners tend to be addicted to control, this feels threatening.

I grew up with the idea that the only way to survive was to be in control and that there was simply no other way to live. Any evidence that I was not in control only served to spur me on to greater efforts. I attempted to control my husband, my children, my house, my career, my garden, and my pets. Most especially, I attempted to control my thoughts, my behavior, and my body. It's no wonder I was seen as tight and cold.

As a result of the physical and emotional tension I generated by holding everything in tight control, I suffered from migraine headaches. They were so painful that I had to seek relief. I tried any number of solutions, moving from traditional to nontraditional approaches in my search. I went to my doctor, a nutritionist, an acupuncturist, and a chiropractor. I tried EST, biofeedback, meditation, yoga, Rolfing, chakra balancing, and past-life regression. From each of these I learned a great deal. I learned that the reliance on control can produce physical pain. I also learned that the desire for control is a result of dependence on what others tell us rather than listening to ourselves.

My discovery that control is unhealthy and even dangerous was not the important insight. It was learning that control results in a strangulation of the ability to live as we were meant to live—fully, wholly, authentically. I realized that when I give up control I am better able to create the life I want.

Giving up control does not equal a naive letting go of responsibility or a "you don't have to do anything and the universe will provide" concept. It is more a substitution of the wisdom of the higher self for control. Using self-knowing instead of mental control challenges us to express ourselves in a way that is in our best interests—*really* best for us and for others.

Giving up the reliance on control has been a long time in coming for me, and it is another of those lessons that may take a lifetime to learn. Every time I let go of controlling a situation, I feel as though I am in danger—that is the way my mind works. And I don't think I am alone in this. Just recently I got another dose of insight on this; sometimes the most trivial incidents prove to be full of learning.

I flew from Denver to Boston to be with my husband, who was there on business, and to visit my children and grandson. My daughter and grandson picked me up at the airport and were to take me to my husband's place of work in the suburbs. He had left the car in the company parking lot and the keys with the receptionist. I was to get the keys from her and drive the car to the hotel. There I would check in and wait for him to be left off by a colleague after a meeting they had attended together.

I had assumed that I would have enough time to get the car keys from the receptionist, even considering Boston traffic. However, it did not turn out as planned. My plane was fifteen minutes late; however, the airline had told my daughter it would be fifty-five minutes late. She arrived twenty minutes later than that, having been held up in traffic. Now we really were in rush hour.

Boston's traffic difficulties are compounded by the fact that to get to the city from the airport everyone must go through a two-lane tunnel. By 5:15 P.M., two hours after I had landed, we were still in the tunnel and I was upset that my daughter had not taken a shortcut or changed lanes to follow a speeding ambulance that left an opening in its wake.

I had realized that my husband's office had closed and I had no access to the car keys. I was worried that my husband and I would wind up at the hotel with no car. For some reason, that possibility loomed as a difficult, time-consuming, and expensive problem to solve, even though I knew that he could get to work the next morning by a $5.00 cab ride.

The real difficulty was that my plan didn't work out and I felt out of control.

We finally gave up on getting to my husband's office and went to pick up my son-in-law at *his* office. It was closer, and by now he was waiting for a ride home. There we went in, got a drink of water, let two-year-old Lyle play for a while, and I left a voice-mail message for my husband regarding my location and the inadvertent change of plans. I finally calmed down enough to remember again that all situations do not have to turn out the way I plan them.

We start to go somewhere with an intention to follow a plan. The important issue is not the plan itself, but that we are doing our business as well as we can while using the situation to become more aware of ourselves and our inner urgings. When we approach life that way, what needs to be done will be done. (Of course, my husband did get the message and the car, and all my worry was needless.)

For some, the awareness of their dharma—their unique way of expressing themselves in the world—will come quickly, as it did for Ellen, who spent years in a computer programming career.

Ellen enjoyed her work, but became aware that she wanted a change. At first, she tried to ignore her thoughts of change, since it would mean starting over, but she knew that she would not be content until she had attended to her deeper yearnings, regardless of the consequences. One day, she suddenly realized she had a desire to work with people in a way that would help them learn and grow. She decided to become a trainer. She began by convincing her boss to let her do some technical training and attend courses that would give her the skills she needed to make a career transition.

Today she is working for a prestigious consulting firm and is a senior management development trainer. Her awareness that she wanted to change careers came to her virtually overnight, but it was the result of a period of quieting her mind in order to allow the solution to arise.

Acceptance

Marcia, who went on a bicycle tour of China (see Chapter Two), struggled briefly but deeply with the acceptance of the message from her higher self. She could not logically explain why she wanted to borrow more money than she imagined she could repay, give up a good job, and go to the other side of the world. Once she made the decision to go, she began to realize that the China tour itself was not really her purpose. Rather, she was giving herself the opportunity to learn about her strengths; she was seeking a larger world to live in; she was giving up her tight control of the small details of her life; she was accepting herself.

One reason we don't easily hear our inner urgings is that they present us with such a challenge. Accepting the wisdom of the higher self generally means living up to our potential, and that can seem pretty scary, especially when we buy into those negative thoughts that we repeat to ourselves.

> Ellen, who is now a management development trainer, had a difficult time following her purpose. She was clear about the new direction she wanted to take, but it was difficult abandoning the years she had invested in her computer career. At first, she couldn't figure out a way to gain the experience and training she would need to carry out her new plan without sacrificing needed income and security. She finally found the courage to tell her boss her dilemma. Her boss responded to Ellen's sincerity and was very supportive. He helped her work out the plan that eventually gave her the experience she needed.

Acceptance of the messages from our higher self works together with our ability to listen to the subconscious. As we allow ourselves to hear our own messages, we are able to perceive more and more of our true knowledge and intuition. Most of us do not allow ourselves to sense more of this wisdom than we can realistically accommodate. The depth of our self may reveal itself in bits and pieces over many years.

Action

Most of us wish we could take more time off to reflect and figure out how to make our lives more meaningful. It is often difficult to see a way to do what we really want. Doing what we want seems formidable because we cannot afford to make the change—after all, how will the bills get paid? And what about our jobs and families? And there certainly are many arrangements that must be made.

> After deciding to make a change in her life, Kathleen waited five years to leave her company, find a part-time job waiting tables, and go back to school to get a law degree. She wanted to be sure her children finished their schooling and became partially self-sufficient before she pursued her own goals. In Kathleen's place, another woman might have attended night school after work in order to make the change earlier; others might never have been able to make the change at all.

There is always a way to do what we really, deeply want to do, even though it may require short-term sacrifices. However, there is nothing wrong with being aware of and accepting an inner call without acting on it. Sometimes waiting is necessary. There will be other chances.

Acting on messages from the higher self can feel exactly like approaching a strange door. Many of us are not able to knock when we get there, but women who have managed to knock usually feel that their lives are fuller, richer, and more satisfying than they were previously. Often the courage to open a strange door comes only when the room we're in becomes too constraining. Effective change is motivated by a sense of purpose, not just by a desire for change for its own sake.

> Carol Lynn is one of the dropouts I interviewed who found the courage to follow her higher self. She worked for several years in the business world, but left to pursue massage therapy. Over time, she evolved into a gifted personal growth counselor. She said, "After years of exploring everything I could do in corporations, I was clear as to what I didn't want to do any more." She took action toward what was right for her, even though it meant a number of years of low income.

Finding the Safety We Need

In *Inner Excellence*, Carol Orsborn (1992) describes the process she followed in accepting the urgings of her higher self and the success she achieved when she used "wanting" as her guide. She describes the process as a spiritual journey, with spirituality defined as "that deeply alive place within each of us that longs for fulfillment." She goes on to describe this process as moving into "the recesses of your own heart . . . to find new sources of inspiration for practical application to your life" (p. 20). She cautions that courage is needed because our society expects and rewards looking outside rather than inside for direction. This is not like the difference between being an extrovert or an introvert. Even an introvert with little access to her subconscious and higher self may gauge her actions by their impact on others. It is following the cultural requirement to obey unthinkingly the rules and hierarchies of our society instead of learning to find and use all aspects of our selves.

Our business world continues to change rapidly, and many of us are being forced to rethink our concept of career safety. Companies are laying off thousands; the skills developed even five years ago may be outdated in the marketplace; and consumer and client needs are changing dramatically. All these changes call into question our reliance on business stability to provide the personal safety we need.

Finding one's inner resources or knowledge will bring with it a sense of safety we can use to proceed, even though we may still need to augment our courage with other techniques. Knowing of others who have accomplished what seems to be the impossible has helped many women to make life changes they knew they needed to make.

Orsborn discovered that she was caught up in the race for greater profits to support a more and more materialistically oriented lifestyle, which was not the direction she deeply wanted to go. She decided to drastically cut back on her business and other commitments outside her home. She sold the expensive house she had just bought and downsized her life. The move gave her the sense of ease and relief that she was seeking—the safety she needed to make the change.

To her surprise, Orsborn then found that her business became even more successful. Giving up the rat race meant having enough time for the fewer projects she did accept. She began to exhibit a sense of wholeness that attracted others.

Self-Alignment for Women

Self-alignment is a human endeavor, not just a feminine one, but it is particularly challenging for women to find themselves—and certainly the masculine nature of the business environment exacerbates the problem.

Our society teaches women, as girls, to follow a set of predetermined rules and to play a prescribed role. The limitations of these rules and roles insert a barrier between women and their true selves. Girls are taught to focus on others and to be caretakers and accommodators; they are taught to respond to the outer world, not to listen for an inner voice. Men, of course, are also taught a prescribed set of behaviors that result in a different set of limitations.

Because most women are the caregivers in their families, it often falls to us to live a life of service to others. When this life style is freely chosen it can be a source of great joy and ever-increasing knowledge that we are accomplishing exactly what we were meant to. Many women, however, neglect themselves, exhibit excessive caregiving, and find themselves playing a role that they feel they have inherited rather than chosen. A life of service must include care of oneself—this is essential. A life of service to others, with this caveat, carries with it the possibility of knowing at the deepest level that we are accomplishing our mission in life, whether we take the time to analyze ourselves or not.

Gloria Steinem, in *Revolution from Within* (1992), speaks about women's need to unlearn the "false self" and find ways to travel inside to learn from the unique knowledge each of us possesses:

Families and cultures that do not foster core self-esteem—and then ration out situational approval in return for obeying, fitting in, servicing the parents' or group's purpose, and doing tasks that are always assigned instead of chosen—produce kids who feel there must be something "wrong" with their own interests and abilities. They therefore begin to create what psychologists call a "false self" in order to earn inclusion and approval, to avoid punishment and ridicule (pp. 66–67).

The women who achieve the greatest measure of self-alignment are those who come closest to both success and fulfillment. Hindsight can work for us. If we comprehend our own patterns, we can choose to change them—or not.

10

The Success Strategies as Paths to Self-Alignment

Self-alignment is critical to finding success and a sense of fulfillment, but achieving it is not easy, and the route differs for those who employ each of the five success strategies. The question that women using any of the strategies must ask themselves is how can they improve their ability to use their inner sense to guide them toward greater self-alignment.

In this chapter, I introduce a chart that summarizes the responses women using each of the success strategies might have to six typical working conditions or situations (see Table 10.1). Following the responses are some "next steps" that might be taken. So, for example, an Emulator like Sarah might find that her response to stress might be to attack or blame others. She might also decide she needs to work even harder. In this case something as simple as breaking the pattern with some exercise, yoga, or even meditation might be useful. She might try biofeedback, a process that trains people to slow their heart rate and generally relax. Scheduling more social time might be all that Sarah could manage.

A Trooper's response to criticism might be to worry about not being as perfect as she believes she should be. This woman might find it useful to ask friends to help sort out what portions of the criticism are valid. It might also be helpful for her to sit down with her manager, spouse, or friend and make a plan to change those personality aspects that the criticism addresses correctly. For a Trooper just to notice the beginning of worry and self-blame is a useful first step.

A Balancer may find that her response to each of these situations feels quite appropriate. For her, the next step is to see if she can use the situation to increase her self-alignment at a deeper level. A Balancer who finds it easy to connect with others at all levels of the organization and who enjoys those relationships may want to understand the nature of those relationships better by, for example, checking her internal response to different situations to see if she is being enriched or depleted. With that knowledge, she can work to include more of the enriching and fewer of the depleting relationships. The differences might be subtle and might require the Balancer to probe beneath her surface expectations. For example, a relationship with a parent or a sibling might be depleting, contrary to her beliefs, while a relationship with a friend or colleague might be particularly enriching.

A Seeker, like Ann, can use any of these situations to learn more about herself; after all, that is what seeking is all about. Seekers might find it interesting to watch their responses to success. Seekers can benefit by asking themselves: Do I accept the credit that is due me, or do I quickly find someone to share it with, as if it were not OK to be recognized? Or do I perhaps grab just a bit more of the credit than is really mine? Any response is a wonderful opportunity to see one's self clearly. Seekers need to remember not to blame themselves for whatever they do, but to notice those reactions that make them feel whole and those that do not.

Integrators are not finished with learning and growing. An Integrator may find herself willing to take on any task that is appropriate to her job, delegate as necessary, and stay focused on the overall goal. All well and good, but there may be benefits to exploring her responses in greater detail. Are there tasks that seem beneath her? Perhaps there are tasks she leaps to take on because she feels particularly comfortable

Table 10.1. Success Strategy Change Matrix.

	EMULATOR	TROOPER	BALANCER	SEEKER	INTEGRATOR
STRESS	RESPONSE Attack, blame, work harder. NEXT STEPS Exercise, biofeedback, yoga, meditation, social time.	RESPONSE Gather more data, work hard, blame self. NEXT STEPS Study effects of stress on your life style; more social time.	RESPONSE Worry, understand cause, look for simple answers. NEXT STEPS Social time, exercise, look at whole life.	RESPONSE Understand, seek personal change. NEXT STEPS Keep larger view, explore tendency to cling to stress.	RESPONSE Understand cause, use stress reduction. NEXT STEPS Explore patterns of stress, focus on whole life goals.
RELATIONSHIPS	RESPONSE Skip personal conversations. NEXT STEPS Ask about others and listen to the answer; tell about yourself.	RESPONSE Rely on friends, show interest and support. NEXT STEPS Explore your value and strengths, relate to yourself.	RESPONSE Enjoy relationships, connect to others. NEXT STEPS Understand when you are depleted, when enriched.	RESPONSE Keep close relationships, seek feedback, support. NEXT STEPS Explore what you give and get, seek reflections on self.	RESPONSE Connect, make self available without "saving" the other. NEXT STEPS Seek self. Explore those who annoy you.
CRITICISM	RESPONSE Outwardly ignore, inwardly increase resolve. NEXT STEPS Identify truth, consider changing.	RESPONSE Worry, blame self. NEXT STEPS Use friends to see what applies, notice worry and self-blame, plan for change.	RESPONSE Identify key issues, plan to resolve. NEXT STEPS Look at your part, consider what you really need to change.	RESPONSE Understand self, look for own contribution. NEXT STEPS Restrain overcriticism, dismiss issues not applicable.	RESPONSE Look at your part, plan to change. NEXT STEPS Explore new behaviors, watch for automatic dismissal.
SUCCESS	RESPONSE Set an even higher goal. NEXT STEPS Enjoy success, notice the part others played, thank them.	RESPONSE Worry, share credit with others. NEXT STEPS Take credit for your part, notice when this feels uncomfortable.	RESPONSE Accept your part, share with others. NEXT STEPS Notice any lack of comfort, explore keeping or giving any credit.	RESPONSE Accept credit, replicate behavior. NEXT STEPS Notice how you feel about self and others.	RESPONSE Accept credit, share; feel motivated to set higher goals. NEXT STEPS Consider your world contribution.
TASK	RESPONSE Work on important tasks, look good. NEXT STEPS Explore your process, look at the cost of looking good.	RESPONSE Accomplish as much as possible; work hard. NEXT STEPS Simplify work, explore cost of accepting all tasks.	RESPONSE Do key tasks, delegate, keep perspective. NEXT STEPS Identify work you truly want to do.	RESPONSE Not driven, will do the necessary. NEXT STEPS Focus on life goals, consider learnings in your work life.	RESPONSE Willing to work, delegate, focus on goal. NEXT STEPS Explore what work means to you.
GOALS	RESPONSE Drive to succeed. NEXT STEPS Study those who have balance and who strive to contribute.	RESPONSE Accomplish all, rely on family to escape. NEXT STEPS Delegate or share work, explore saying no, explore self.	RESPONSE Plan and monitor best approach. NEXT STEPS Consider how goals fit into your whole life.	RESPONSE Succeed, with focus on personal goals. NEXT STEPS Explore response to goals of others.	RESPONSE Put goal in perspective; accomplish other goals if possible. NEXT STEPS Consider life goals, business goals, focus on congruency.

doing them. Any response can help the Integrator to look deeper into what "work" means to her: What kind of work is good? Why? Who says? Integrators may find that they do certain tasks because they are easy and others applaud when they are completed. To what extent is the Integrator controlling the way she appears to others so they will approve of her? Does she need their approval? Why?

The value of Table 10.1 is in creating awareness, not in finding a pigeonhole. You may find that you have the response of a Trooper in one situation and that of a Seeker in another. This chart was created to stimulate your thought process regarding the steps you choose to take.

As we explore possible next steps for each of the success strategies, keep in mind the three elements of discovering and expressing self-alignment: acceptance, awareness, and action. I'll describe each strategy in those terms.

Paths to Self-Alignment for the Emulator

A young woman recently pleaded, "Help. I'm an Emulator. What do I do?" Unwittingly, she had already taken her first step toward self-alignment by acknowledging that the way she was acting was not getting her what she wanted in life. Her observation is critical to any Emulator who wants to make a change. Becoming aware of any misalignment is the same thing as identifying the first step on the path toward greater self-alignment.

The second step in change is acceptance—acceptance of self, acceptance of a need for change, and acceptance of external realities. Acceptance does not mean giving up all masculine business skills that have been so hard won. The business world will never operate on a totally feminine basis, whatever that might mean. The business culture is, however, moving toward a more balanced style and developing the flexibility to appreciate and make use of multiple differences.

I once had a manager, Karen, who had a strong personality and had developed a rather brusque business style. For some reason

(I never asked her why) she came to the realization that she had eliminated most traces of her femininity. She decided that she would feel better about herself if she made an effort to remind herself of the feminine side of her nature.

In her efforts to change, Karen had her hair done in a softer style and began to get a manicure every week. She also began to acknowledge when she was upset, whether by a personal setback or by an employee's personal crisis. I even saw her in tears once when her usually competent secretary made some errors and finally confessed that she had just put her father in a nursing home because he had Alzheimer's disease. Despite her feminization, Karen continued to be an extremely successful manager who was responsible for a major portion of company revenue. In accepting herself, Karen did not detract from her ability to make hard decisions or confront inferior performance.

For Emulators, acceptance can seem like a bit of a double bind. If they have the confidence to accept themselves as they are, they are already self-aligned in some measure. Without confidence in themselves, self-acceptance is extremely difficult. The problem is that confidence can *only* come from within. It is impossible to find a sense of self by looking outside for judgment or approval. It is only by looking inside that we find the inner resolve to exhibit our true selves—and so, full circle, we are faced with the issue of "revolution from within," as Steinem labeled it. To find acceptance, the Emulator must nourish the perhaps dimly felt sense that she is more than her performance at work and that she would like more from her life.

When Emulators seek change, they, more than women using the other strategies, want a set of actions they can follow. They want the process to be neat and clean and precise. They are generally impatient with fuzzy concepts, long-term processes, and with "being" rather than "doing." Yet, in order to change to another role and increase self-alignment, Emulators must confront these concepts. The process *is* fuzzy, it *will* take time, and *being* in addition to *doing* creates success. Awareness, acceptance, and then action.

Sometimes a small step toward acceptance can be a critical one in hindsight. Acknowledging her femininity by having her nails done every week was the small step Karen took. Some Emulators may start to change just by resolving to examine feedback that they are difficult or harsh or cold. Several ex-Emulators told me that it was the little "moments of truth" that started them off in a different direction. For others, it was the accumulated evidence that something was just not working—that things would get better only if they changed. They finally realized that the world was not going to do the changing for them. Emulators can act to change, but first they have to become aware of and accepting of themselves; only then will they know how to act.

Paths to Self-Alignment for the Trooper

The Trooper is likely to know a change is needed, yet lack the courage to actually make the change. For the Trooper, action is the difficult step. Troopers often see that the way they act is not going to get them what they want, yet they continue to act that way because they cannot conceive of any but unpalatable alternatives. Accepting a need to change implies a search for alternatives that are acceptable and at the same time effective. Troopers assume that because they can't imagine a reasonable option for themselves, none exists.

The action step for Troopers is dependent upon expanding their creativity and allowing themselves to consider alternatives they haven't considered before. Next, they have to try out the new behavior. They must be sure to provide enough safety for themselves in the process to make the changes possible. Using small steps may be the way to make change and still feel safe.

Troopers are often guided by examples set by others and by encouragement from friends and family. Consciously collecting stories of women who do the things Troopers only dream of doing can be motivating. It helps to identify the first steps others have taken to make the change seem within the realm of possibility for the Trooper.

Mary, who is a Trooper, was buried in academia in the Northeast and decided that her job was not satisfying enough; she dreamed of change. Since she had to support herself, she did not believe that she could start over. Mary's job paid well and she was competent enough that she could do what was expected with little extra effort. As a safe way to initiate the change she desired, she took a course on massage and started a massage therapy practice in her off hours. She continued to work at her job at the university and found increased satisfaction even there. This small change in her life has given her great personal satisfaction and has opened the door for even greater change in the future.

Another woman, Carmela, began to realize that her excessive attention to every detail was creating more work than she could reasonably do, and generating such stress that she began to have severe headaches. In an attempt to relieve the pain, she began to explore stress-reduction methods. This opened up several avenues for her. One was a management course that taught her how to delegate better and yet keep track of how the delegated work was progressing. She had previously believed that she either had to do the work herself or lose control of it entirely.

A second stress-reduction technique was a yoga class Carmela reluctantly attended, only to find that this gentle series of stretches and movements helped her to feel so much better physically that she was able to bring greater energy to her work and to the management techniques she was learning. In the process of this learning, her headaches diminished significantly and she was given a promotion and a raise.

Mary and Carmela accepted their need for change and started with small, safe changes. In both cases, the changes led to significant increases in their feelings of physical well-being and self-esteem.

Even such small steps toward expressing themselves increase self-alignment for Troopers. If they continue changing, they will find that self-alignment itself provides the feeling of safety they cherish. The safety itself can encourage Troopers to keep discovering and expressing their unique personalities in the world.

Paths to Self-Alignment for the Balancer

The issue for the Balancer is the same as for the Emulator: awareness. As we have seen, Balancers are often quite satisfied with the extent to which they have learned to thrive in the business world. For them, there may be no sense of dissatisfaction and no urge to increase self-alignment. Thus, not all Balancers will want to change. But many Balancers do sense that they could have more or that there is something wrong. They often ignore their internal warning signal because they have created a life style that works well for them and it is hard for them to imagine adding something to an already full and precariously balanced life.

Self-alignment is not something *more*, however. It is not just another activity to be added to a Balancer's three-page, single-spaced to-do list. It is not another element to add to one's personality, but rather a deepening of one's character; it is more akin to a discovery than to an addition. Discovering that one lives in a maze of false concepts and expectations is not an activity that can be added to or checked off a list. A desire for "something more" that a Balancer might ignore—for fear that it might be the proverbial straw—can also be a wake-up call to an easier life. The key for the Balancer is becoming aware of her internal signal. Once she hears it, she will act on it. Balancers are great at action.

And exploring ways to increase self-alignment can be fun—like Forrest Gump's box of chocolates—you don't know *what* you will find. It is not something that one has to, or can, study in an intellectual way. Allowing ourselves to become aware of our desire for a fuller, deeper, richer, and easier life starts us on a path toward self-discovery that enriches any life.

Paths to Self-Alignment for the Seeker

The Seeker starts out with a general awareness that she is not as honest with herself as she could be or would like to be. She often finds it difficult to express this to others, since there seems to be no language for her search. The only similar process she knows of is the efforts of those seeking to diminish emotional distress. Some Seekers do try the therapeutic route. While this can be quite helpful for relinquishing old behaviors, therapy typically does not address the more spiritual forms of discontent. It is not that something is wrong, but that it is not quite right; and there is a vast difference between the two. In fact, nothing *is* wrong. The Seeker is actually motivated by the possibility that there is a great deal more to be discovered in life; that there are enriching and broadening possibilities.

For the Seeker, the area of self-alignment that provides the greatest difficulty is the action phase. The problems lie in two areas: The Seeker may halt after the acceptance stage and not be able to carry through on her changes; or conversely, she may devote herself entirely to change, losing perspective on the rest of her life.

The first of these problems is akin to applying the Trooper perspective to the Seeker role. That is, the Seeker may become engrossed in the process of collecting all possible information about herself in order to be sure that she makes the right decision about changing, and never get around to making the changes.

The second pitfall, loss of perspective, occurs when, in the intensity of the search, some Seekers inadvertently exchange their feminine, holistic view for a more masculine and linear approach. They attack their journey with the expectation that they can discover everything about themselves at once and instantly transform their lives.

> Shirley, a Seeker who ran into problems, was captivated by the discovery that she was an introvert. She had never realized why she preferred small groups to large ones or reveled in quiet time alone or why she preferred to mull things over before she was sure of her opinion. This one self-discovery made her feel so much better about herself that she was determined to discover more. She became consumed by lectures, seminars, and workshops that

promised to deliver personality insights. While she actually got very little from some of these guided explorations, she was always enthusiastic about the possibilities they offered. In between group activities, she read pop psych books, jotted down her dreams, and kept a journal. She was sure that what she was learning about herself would improve other aspects of her life.

Shirley became so consumed with her self-explorations that her attention to her job began to falter. Finally, her boss told her that the members of the small group she managed were being assigned to take over the accounts of the various clients they served. She was being transferred to another section, where she would report to a man who had been her colleague. Astonished, she asked why. She was told that her clients had become frustrated with trying to get her to assume a strategic role and each had lobbied her boss to change things.

Shirley, who was ambitious, was devastated by this blow to her career. She got the message about keeping her priorities straight, quickly refocused on her job, and was soon promoted. She did not completely abandon her interest in self-exploration, but she did learn to place it in perspective and to spread out the events she attended. Ironically, she discovered that slowing her pace increased her ability to internalize new discoveries.

For the Seeker, the process of self-alignment deepens the communication with her higher self and empowers her to make choices about her life; her outer world will begin to show evidence of an inner congruence. The key ingredient in moving toward greater self-alignment is action. The Seeker must be careful not to be stopped by fear or to overemphasize the process.

Paths to Self-Alignment for the Integrator

Integrators are not perfectly aligned each moment of the day or even every day. They have, however, acquired the skills to realign themselves when they slip out of focus. Becoming aligned with ourselves is not something we achieve, like winning the softball league title or getting a promotion. It is more like learning a new language: If we don't practice it regularly, we may retain a few words, but we will forget the syntax and lose our ability to converse. Self-alignment requires diligence and practice, but it does not feel like hard work.

There are people who are so attracted to the Integrator's inner strength that they cling to her in order to feel complete. The Integrator's clear decision is to live fully while expressing all of her skills and attributes. This may mean choosing to have little to do with those who diminish her sense of self, either by their envy or their desire to attach themselves to her.

The Integrator, like any of us, may occasionally question her value or skills or intelligence, but she is generally able to use the questioning as a trigger to renew her self-alignment. For the Integrator, self-alignment is generally a matter of awareness; awareness of when she slips into a negative pattern. Acceptance and action are usually not problematic for the Integrator, as long as she remembers who she is.

PART FOUR

Changing the Business Environment

11

Coming Full Circle: A Fresh View of the Organizational Challenge

If we wish to find out what works, we must start with our own values and personal situation. Management is best conceived as constructive self-fulfilling prophecies, acting in ways to make happen what we most believe in.

—Marvin Weisbord

I began my quest by asking why organizations were training their employees in feminine attributes and skills yet were often not "woman friendly." Seeking an answer to this paradox led me to an understanding of the success strategies women use to deal with the common business environment and the power of finding and expressing oneself in an authentic way.

Being true to oneself is a key ingredient in finding business success; it is also the most important aspect of developing a keen sense of joy and fulfillment in life. As we have seen, however, developing self-alignment in the context of the business world is no easy task for most. The question now arises, having put time, attention, and energy into the pursuit of self-alignment, what can we do to encourage our organizations to value authenticity over artifice? How can we create "alignment friendly" organizations?

Women *are* in the process of changing today's society, including the business sector, by bringing themselves into focus as whole people. In so doing, they are "building a new reality, a new social order or paradigm," as Patricia Aburdene and John Naisbitt illustrate in depth in *Megatrends*

177

for Women (1992). This new order is a partnership along the lines set forth by Riane Eisler in *The Chalice and the Blade* (1987), wherein both women and men work together, exploring and expressing their unique potentials.

If the business world is to keep up with the social change, it is time for business leaders to start altering their environments to reflect the principles of collaboration, teamwork, human concern, and intuition— to start valuing the feminine attributes. To the extent that they are leaders, women and forward-thinking men can influence organizations by policy making and by example. It is no coincidence that these new business qualities are being espoused at the same time that women are inching up the corporate ladder in significant numbers.

There are three reasons for the timelines of this change: First, numerous experts indicate that corporations require new skills to survive. Read, for example, Marvin Weisbord's compelling book *Productive Workplaces* (1987). He states that "new methods are needed to realize our values and keep businesses viable" (p. 253). Joseph Boyett and Henry Conn in *Workplace 2000* (1992) provide examples of the diversity of workers and skills that will be required in the future.

Second, workers are demanding greater personal control over their destinies. Orsburn, Moran, Musselwhite, and Zenger in *Self-Directed Work Teams* (1990) summarize the current wave of empowerment and illustrate the value of relying on workers to make the right business decisions.

And finally, women are already changing their worlds, as Patricia Aburdene and John Naisbitt (1992) show in detail. Women are increasing their numbers in most professions. More important, the business world is rapidly becoming "feminized," as illustrated by the growth in dependence on such behaviors as collaboration, teamwork, interpersonal skills, and care and concern for the customer and product. These three forces are combining to generate more humanizing and democratic work environments.

Companies and their employees can prosper by operating in accord with more feminine characteristics. Aburdene and Naisbitt provide examples to show that the feminine style of leadership also induces greater productivity. The "new culture" is not just about being nicer; it incorporates a true balance of the best feminine and masculine approaches to managing business and people. Author Joline Godfrey (1992) has also studied women-owned and women-run businesses. She has found that they are successful in traditional balance sheet terms and that they demonstrate how to treat and keep valuable employees as well as positively impact the global environment.

Fighting the Status Quo

Despite widespread support for a more humanized business landscape, change has a powerful enemy that can slow, and in some companies obliterate, its progress. The enemy is the status quo. Many executives and other business leaders find themselves unable to change their companies *even when they themselves advocate adopting the new values*. They even find it difficult to change themselves. Status quo is a powerful rubber band; it tends to snap back to its original shape unless it is held for long enough in the new position.

Organizational change can happen in two ways: It can start at the top (but it must be actively supported from the top in order to work its way down), or it can occur at the individual level. Ultimately, the two methods must combine for the change to be both effective and permanent.

Top-Down Change

General Electric offers an example of a change effort being driven from the top. CEO Jack Welsh personally and vigorously engineered the sweeping changes he saw as essential to the survival of GE. He instituted a drive for excellence by demanding that each division rank at the top of its particular market. By this edict, he created radical changes throughout the company. He has, thereby, been successful at revitalizing an old-style company.

In too many companies, change efforts consume massive quantities of time and money and still fail. Change efforts fail when senior man-agement (and, by example, the rest of their employees) reverts to the old familiar routine, thereby undermining their own efforts. Most change efforts are not supported by a corresponding change in culture, so the only operating norms shared by executives and employees are the old ones. Under stress, it is easier to employ the familiar than to work to bring about new norms and principles that will support the change effort. It is not (usually) that business people are contrary; it is more that they have no clear picture of the new style. Building and culturally expressing a vision of the future is the job of senior management, and this is where Welsh has been so effective. He continues to explain where GE is going, to set an example of the new style, and to generate trust in the future among his people.

> As a consultant, I was involved with a change effort in the banking industry. The analysis by the reengineers was brilliant, senior man-agement was convinced, and the change effort began to take shape. Pilot branch offices, operating in the new way, were estab-lished across the country. Branch office personnel were coached for months on new methods, such as focusing on marketing, flat-tening of the organization structure, and utilizing an information system that provided accurate analysis of risk factors. The key to success was to be the careful implementation of self-managing teams. The coaching included support to help shift attitudes and behaviors. In a short time, the new method began to show the hoped-for financial results.
>
> In their excitement over the early success, senior management decided to implement the changes nationwide, far ahead of the recommended time schedule. They saw the recommendation to allow time for employees to adapt to the attitudinal changes as unnecessary. Management believed that the structural changes, along with increased pressure to achieve higher profit margins, would be sufficient to force the change through.

Underlying management's excitement were three unspoken rationales that actually drove their decision. First, and most important, the stock price had fallen and it was felt that immediate improvement of the financial picture would drive it back up again. Second, the management team did not comprehend the need to provide time and support for the psychological change process to occur. Third, there was an unspoken recognition that the change would result in a loss of control by those who had power under the old system. To a person, the senior management team reverted to two old business standbys: command-and-control and ready-fire-aim, both totally at odds with the team decision-making process they were ostensibly trying to implement.

By rushing the change effort and by choosing to have all decisions made at the highest levels, management effectively destroyed the project's chances for success.

It is only when people at senior levels remain consciously aware of the far-reaching impact of their actions, and model new behaviors accordingly, that they can enable their organizations to successfully implement organizational changes.

Individual Pressure

Organizational change can occur at the individual level. In Chapter Two, I described how individuals can create microclimates of authenticity around themselves. When the microclimates of numerous individuals interact, they can combine into a powerful force for change that can affect a whole organization. The combining of microclimates is similar to the principle of reaching critical mass, a term from physics that describes the process of combining radioactive fuel to produce a nuclear reaction. Once critical mass is achieved, the reaction becomes self-sustaining. The principle of critical mass applies equally well to social change, as can be seen in the success of many grassroots movements that have brought about political change.

One positive business development that has come about due to the critical mass principle is the improvement of child care policies. Women who left the workforce to bear and raise their children cost companies millions of dollars that had been invested in training and promoting female employees. Businesses learned that it was cheaper to provide pregnancy leave and child care support than to lose their trained workers.

Another type of change is happening at the individual level because workers want to know more about their jobs than simply what their duties are. They want decision-making power over the variable aspects of their jobs. Assembly line workers, for example, prefer to be able to choose whether they will meet their quota in the morning and do preventive maintenance in the afternoon, or vice versa. Workers' desire for a greater say in their own daily activities has led companies to look to such programs as team building, empowerment, joint goal setting, and big picture communications to provide workers more input and greater personal power.

Given the evidence of change already taking place and my own experience and research, I believe that women and men as individuals will be able to influence the prevailing business paradigm—to succeed, and feel a complete sense of fulfillment—by moving consciously toward self-alignment. By integrating ourselves, we can do our part to create a business environment that honors us for what we know, who we are, and how our unique presence and perspective contribute to the whole. Each of us has a role to play in creating a new style of business partnership. We need to participate both as individuals and as leaders or members of our organizations.

A Systemic View

Let us look at what happens when women act more in balance with themselves and when they consciously seek to increase the amount of self-alignment they can call on in their business dealings.

I will use a simple technique taken from a discipline called systems

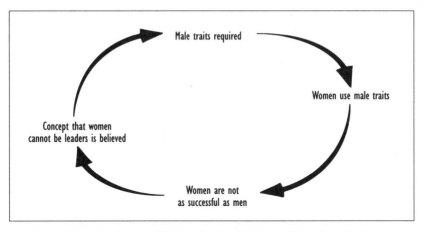

Figure 11.1. The Systems Thinking Model with Women Using Masculine Traits in Business.

thinking, which provides a way of analyzing a situation by identifying the major interrelationships and patterns rather than by focusing on separate parts or events. (For a more detailed explanation, I suggest Peter Senge's 1990 book, *The Fifth Discipline*. Even for those who are not interested in systems thinking, it is a powerful way to look at change in organizations today.)

Systems thinking is expressed best in diagrams that show the reinforcing and negating forces inherent in a system. In Figure 11.1, arrows represent the connections and influences of the forces. The arrows are equivalent to cause and effect statements. See what happens when systems thinking is applied to the question of whether self-aligned women can change the business climate.

In business, there is a prevailing belief that certain traits generally defined as masculine (assertiveness, single-minded focus on the goal, reliance on hierarchy, and so forth) are required for success. In our culture these traits are the ones most associated with task accomplishment. In fact, we have little language and few models to illustrate the ways in which other traits (concern for relationships, a sense of the whole, the ability to let events unfold, and so forth) also lead to effective accomplishment.

As a result of this pervasive belief, women who want to succeed learn to exaggerate their own masculine traits. It is generally accepted by both men and women that women have not been as successful as they ought to be given their obvious skill and determination. This observation has resulted in the conviction that women cannot be counted on for the really important jobs. In a beautiful example of circular logic, this conviction reinforces the original notion that masculine traits are required for business success.

Figure 11.1 illustrates the premise that masculine traits are required for success in business. The arrow leading from this conceptual element of the system signifies the positive connection between it and the fact that many women utilize masculine attributes, or at least the attributes they think men have. The next arrow indicates that women who use exclusively male traits are not as successful as men in the long run. (For example, in Chapter Four it was shown that Emulators are held back because of their overuse of masculine traits. One might argue that women using feminine traits are also not as successful as men. However, in Chapter Two it was shown that an increase in women's self alignment does increase the probability for success.)

The idea that women are not successful reinforces the concept that women cannot be leaders, which in turn reinforces the original idea that masculine traits are required. Here is how we get the reinforcing circle that perpetuates the old-style masculine status quo in our business culture.

Of course there are other factors involved in maintaining the notion that male traits are required, but the element we want to consider is women using male traits. For instance, what happens when women use male traits but augment them with their own feminine attributes (collaboration, sharing credit, and the like)? (See Figure 11.2.)

Many women find it impossible to use male traits exclusively. When women use a balance of masculine and feminine skills and traits,

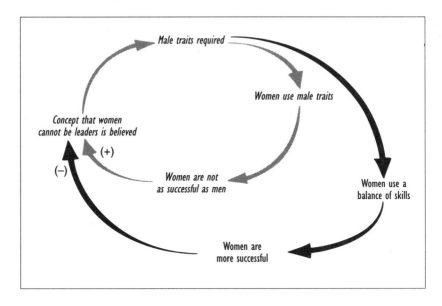

Figure 11.2. The Systems Thinking Model with Women Using a Balance of Skills.

they are more successful than when they use only masculine ones. Again, we see support for this point in the writings of Aburdene and Naisbitt (1992), Helgesen (1990), Sargent (1983), and Schwartz (1992).

Showing that one element of the diagram is untrue—women are not as successful as men—calls into question the other elements: that women cannot be leaders and thus that male traits are required. The original circle is kept, but there is now another set of factors that result in negating the concept that women cannot be leaders. When women use a balance of feminine and masculine skills, they are more successful than when using masculine skills alone.

To follow the forces in Figure 11.2, first locate the original circle and then turn to the new loop that has been added to it. In the first loop, male traits are used exclusively. In the added loop, women use a balance of male and female skills and women are more successful. The fact that women are more successful begins to negate the concept that women cannot be leaders (hence the minus sign). Now there are two opposing forces operating on the concept that women cannot be leaders, one a supporting force and the other a negating force. The negating force places *pressure* on the concept that women cannot be leaders, but it does not dispel it. Using a balance of traits is a good start, and for many women, it is probably the best they can do. However, there is more.

As women are more successful in using a balance of skills, many find they are naturally interested in increasing self-alignment. As shown in Chapters Nine and Ten, when women improve self-alignment, they acquire more competence and confidence, which provide them an increased sense of fulfillment and greater success. Adding this to the diagram places even greater pressure on the concept that women cannot be leaders (or ought not be in business in the first place).

In Figure 11.3, locate the original circle and move from "male traits required" to "women use a balance of skills." Using a balance of skills makes women more successful, but this is not enough to break down the original idea that male traits are required, so we add another set of forces. Women who find greater success using a balance of skills often find that they naturally start to increase self-alignment. As we saw in the descriptions of the Balancer, Seeker, and Integrator, women who display more competence and confidence (owing to their greater self-alignment) become more successful. This increased success places an additional negating force on the concept that women cannot be leaders, and the combination of negating forces begins to break down the masculine business status quo.

This succession of diagrams shows how women are able to change the business culture just through their willingness to search for and exhibit their own inner wisdom. By combining women's (and men's) microclimates of authenticity and self-alignment, women can create changes in the larger business environment.

The business changes that self-aligned women bring about are similar to what business leaders are attempting to create with projects and training in teamwork, networking, and collaboration and by intro-

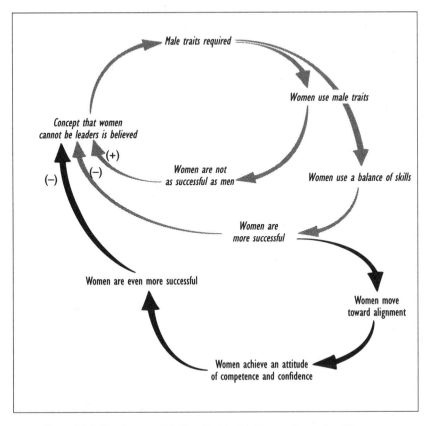

Figure 11.3. The Systems Thinking Model with Women Increasing Alignment.

ducing other feminine styles into the workplace. Management is interested in these changes because of their potential for increasing productivity and revenues. Management is starting to understand that using each individual's potential to the fullest is the best route to these increases. Businesswomen are not the only ones to benefit from change. There are many men who function in the old style in order to survive who find relief in the feminizing changes.

We have previously confirmed that increasing self-alignment plays a major role in a woman's personal success and life fulfillment.

Now we see that seeking self-alignment also has a positive impact on our business environment. This is clearly an important topic for future exploration.

Feminine Pride

Women are starting to experience a new sense of pride. Their denunciations and rage are lessening, and there is more emphasis on a new spirit of partnership. The concern now is how women can express themselves in ways that lead both to material success and to inner fulfillment. There is less emphasis on how to convince men to change. These shifts are making it easier for men to comprehend and respond to the new approach to feminine concerns. Men are also feeling the winds of change and looking to find a greater balance within themselves.

Now that women are beginning to claim their own power, the focus is on how to find success and integrity in the workplace. It is not easy. The business environment is changing very slowly.

Some companies recognize that they suffer a loss when women drop out, and they are making the effort to become more inviting to women. Organizations that consciously move to a more balanced stance have demonstrated that material success can be an outcome or corollary of being "woman friendly." Many men have also worked for and achieved balanced skills. Many others, however, are unaware of the tremendous value of diversity (including others besides women). They miss opportunities to use the best balance of skills around them. Old-style managers will find themselves changing, however, in the natural course of events.

The question this book has posed is, how can women achieve the success they want and keep themselves whole in the process? Women must prepare themselves for success by learning the business, gaining leadership skills, and networking with business allies. It is also helpful to recognize that being respected and being liked are not the same. In business, respect counts. It is also useful to realize that some elements of the business environment will remain "masculine" for good business reasons.

For some women, success will continue to be defined as just having a job and raising a family. Other women will strive for a greater sense of balance in their lives; they will seek challenge and respect in the workplace. They will want an opportunity to make a difference, and they will also want time for their loved ones.

A final group of women will want more. They will want to explore the relationship between who they are and how they act in every aspect of their lives. They will be constantly challenged from within to express congruence in thought, word, and action. They will see that people who have that congruence have a natural power that is truly a balance of feminine and masculine, and they will want that for themselves.

In doing the research that led to this book, I have been tremendously moved by the courage of working women—women who have tried hard to do the right thing, to be successful, to do a good job, to fit in, and to belong. Unfortunately, their struggles may not get them what they really want, which is respect, consideration, acknowledgment, responsibility, authority, promotions, and opportunities to contribute to the best of their abilities.

We can change our society, including the workplace, so that it will value a balance of feminine and masculine attributes in both men and women. In my view, this would result in a much more efficient and effective use of the working population. I have suggested a few actions we can all take. There is obviously much work to be done in this regard.

I have attempted to hold up a mirror to the workplace in an effort to encourage both men and women to consider their journey toward themselves. We cannot choose to change the pattern until we comprehend it. When we take charge of our own decisions, we reap increased measures of self-determination, and that guides us toward our own personal truth.

In presenting this mirror to the business world, I speak the truth for myself and, I hope, for many women and men.

Bibliography

Aburdene, Patricia, and Naisbitt, John. *Megatrends for Women: From Liberation to Leadership*. New York: Fawcett Columbine, 1992.

Barrentine, Pat, ed. *When the Canary Stops Singing*. San Francisco: Berrett-Koehler, 1993.

Block, Peter. *Stewardship: Choosing Service Over Self-Interest*. San Francisco: Berrett-Koehler, 1993.

Boyett, Joseph H., and Conn, Henry P. *Workplace 2000*. New York: Plume, 1992.

Bradshaw, John. *Healing the Shame That Binds You*. Deerfield Beach, Fla.: Health Communications, 1988.

Bridges, William. *Transitions: Making Sense of Life's Changes*. Reading, Mass.: Addison-Wesley, 1980.

Cornwall, Susan. "Culture and Work-Life Programs: Assessing and Fostering Readiness and Commitment." Paper presented at the Work and Life Conference, Boston, April 1993.

Cox, Meg. "Business Books Emphasize the Spiritual." *Wall Street Journal*, Dec. 14, 1992.

Dass, Ram. *Journey of Awakening*. New York: Bantam Books, 1978.

Dass, Ram. *Spiritual Awakening*. Niles, Ill.: Nightingale Conant, 1993. (Audio program.)

Eisler, Riane. *The Chalice and the Blade*. New York: Harper & Row, 1987.

Faludi, Susan. *Backlash*. New York: Crown, 1991.

Fritz, Robert. *DMA Course Manual*. Cambridge, Mass.: Dimensional Mind Approach, 1980.

Fritz, Robert. *The Path of Least Resistance*. New York: Fawcett Columbine, 1989.

Gilligan, Carol. *In a Different Voice*. Cambridge, Mass.: Harvard University Press, 1982.

Godfrey, Joline. *Our Wildest Dreams*. New York: HarperBusiness, 1992.

Gray, John. *Men Are from Mars, Women Are from Venus*. New York: HarperCollins, 1992.

Hancock, Emily. *The Girl Within*. New York: Fawcett Columbine, 1989.

Harman, Willis. *Global Mind Change*. Indianapolis, Ind.: Knowledge Systems, Inc., 1988.

Harman, Willis, and Rheingold, Howard. *Higher Creativity*. Los Angeles: Tarcher, 1984.

Heider, John. *The Tao of Leadership*. New York: Bantam Books, 1985.

Heilbrun, Carolyn G. *Reinventing Womanhood*. New York: Norton, 1979.

Helgesen, Sally. *The Female Advantage*. New York: Doubleday/Currency, 1990.

Jamieson, David, and O'Mara, Julie. *Managing Workforce 2000*. San Francisco: Jossey-Bass, 1991.

Kanter, Rosabeth M. *Men and Women of the Corporation*. New York: Basic Books, 1977.

Karpinski, Gloria D. *Where Two Worlds Touch*. New York: Ballantine Books, 1990.

Krebs, Nina Boyd. *Changing Woman Changing Work*. Aspen, Colo.: MacMurray and Beck, 1993.

Kroeger, Otto, with Thuesen, Janet M. *Type Talk at Work*. New York: Delacorte Press, 1992.

Lewan, Lloyd S. *Women in the Workplace: A Man's Perspective*. Boulder, Colo.: Johnson, 1988.

Luft, Joseph. *Of Human Interaction*. Palo Alto, Calif.: National Press Books, 1969.

Mason, Marilyn. *Making Our Lives Our Own*. New York: HarperCollins, 1991.

McCallum, Pat. *Stepping Free of Limiting Patterns*. Chevy Chase, Md.: Source Unlimited, 1992.

Moir, Anne, and Jessel, David. *Brain Sex*. New York: Doubleday, 1989.

Morrison, Ann; White, Randall; VanVelson, Ellen; and the Center for Creative Leadership. *Breaking the Glass Ceiling: Can Women Reach the Top of America's Largest Corporations?* Reading, Mass.: Addison-Wesley, 1992.

Nelson, Martia. *Coming Home: The Return to True Self*. Mill Valley, Calif.: Nataraj, 1993.

Nickerson, Jan. "Helping Your Dream Job Find You." In *When the Canary Stops Singing*, Pat Barrentine, ed. San Francisco: Berrett-Koehler, 1993.

Orsborn, Carol. *Inner Excellence*. San Rafael, Calif.: New World Library, 1992.

Orsburn, Jack D.; Moran, Linda; Musselwhite, ed; and Zenger, John H. *Self-Directed Work Teams*. Homewood, Ill.: Business One Irwin, 1990.

Patent, Arnold M. *You Can Have It All*. Sylva, N.C.: Celebration Publishing, 1991.

Powell, Gary N. *Women and Men in Management*. Newbury Park, Calif.: Sage, 1988.

Rogers, Carl R. *On Becoming a Person*. Boston: Houghton Mifflin, 1961.

Sargent, Alice G. *The Androgynous Manager*. New York: American Management Associations, 1983.

Schaef, Anne Wilson. *Women's Reality*. New York: Harper & Row, 1981.

Schwartz, Felice. *Breaking with Tradition*. New York: Warner Books, 1992.

Senge, Peter M. *The Fifth Discipline: The Art and Practice of the Learning Organization*. New York: Doubleday Currency, 1990.

Sinetar, Marsha. *Do What You Love, the Money Will Follow*. New York: Dell, 1987.

Singer, June. *Seeing Through the Visible World*. San Francisco: Harper & Row, 1990.

Sogyal, Rinpoche. *The Tibetan Book of Living and Dying*. San Francisco: HarperCollins, 1992.

Steinem, Gloria. *Revolution from Within: A Book of Self-Esteem*. Boston: Little, Brown, 1992.

Tannen, Deborah. *You Just Don't Understand: Women and Men in Conversation*. New York: Ballantine Books, 1990.

Tavris, Carol. *The Mismeasure of Woman*. New York: Simon & Schuster, 1992.

Weisbord, Marvin R. *Productive Workplaces*. San Francisco: Jossey-Bass, 1987.

Williamson, Marianne. *A Woman's Worth*. New York: Random House, 1993.

Index

The Author

NANCY H. BANCROFT is the cofounder of Bancroft, Brite & Associates, Inc., a management consulting and training firm. She speaks, consults, and writes about the human and organizational aspects of change. Currently she is focused on the role played by self-alignment in generating both success in the workplace and a sense of fulfillment in life.

Nancy has an varied and integrated background. She started her career as a systems analyst and worked for ten years as a manager and consultant in the computer systems field. During this period, she decided to complete an M.B.A. degree in organizational development— a turning point in her career. For the next ten years, she worked as an OD (organization development) consultant, specializing in sociotechnical systems design. She has developed and delivered numerous management development training courses and is noted for her ability to facilitate intact work groups.

Nancy has been actively committed to pursuing her own personal growth for twenty years. She explores spirituality, the "new" sciences, perennial philosophy, and women's studies. She works with the aging and dying as a volunteer in her local hospice organization.

Nancy earned her A.B. degree from the College of William and Mary and her M.B.A. degree from Clark University. She has also completed the Columbia University advanced program in organization development and human resource management.

Nancy drew on her technical, business, and organization experiences in writing her first book, New Partnerships for Managing Technological Change (Wiley, 1992).

Nancy can be contacted at 1153 Evergreen Parkway, Suite M-469, Evergreen, Colorado 80439, phone (303) 670-8253.